America's Yesterdays

America's

Yesterdays

Images of our lost past
discovered in the photographic archives
of the Library of Congress

by **Oliver Jensen**

Published by
AMERICAN HERITAGE PUBLISHING CO., INC., New York
Book Trade Distribution by SIMON and SCHUSTER, New York

Photographic Research Shirley L. Green

Design Nelson Gruppo

RIGHT: In 1885, a full year before Bartholdi's Statue of Liberty lifted her lamp beside the golden door, a New York photographer named B. J. Falk had copyrighted his own version, a composite featuring the wrong part of the harbor and an actress named Ramie Austen—inspiring and suitable for framing.

FRONT ENDPAPER: This uncaptioned, enigmatic scene taken by Charles M. Currier shows someone's old homestead near Boston in the 1890's. Who are the two families? Who is the seated old lady? Is the place being sold? No one knows.

HALF-TITLE PAGE: Like many "transfers" to the Library of Congress, this came from the Department of Agriculture bare of information. But it tells its own story.

TITLE PAGE: News photography was coming into its own when Frances Benjamin Johnston's camera caught the photographers' stand for the second inaugural parade of President William McKinley in 1901.

BACK ENDPAPER: It is 1907, and we are looking down Fifth Avenue; from the lack of traffic, the well-dressed children, and the angle of the shadows, it must be Sunday morning. The two high buildings, the St. Regis Hotel at left and the Gotham Hotel at right, and the Presbyterian church in front of the latter are still there. But almost everything else is gone, including the huge Vanderbilt mansion at right, in front of whose gates a touring car with its clouds of fumes provides intimations of a noxious future.

AMERICAN HERITAGE BOOKS
Editor-in-chief Ezra Bowen

Staff for **AMERICA'S YESTERDAYS**
Text Editor Richard F. Snow
Copy Editor Beatrice Gottlieb
Researchers Jane Colihan, Myra M. Mangan
Art Assistant Robin Kenny

AMERICAN HERITAGE PUBLISHING CO., INC.
Chairman of the Board Samuel P. Reed
President and Publisher Rhett Austell
Art Director Murray Belsky
Subsidiary Rights Director Beverley Hilowitz

Library of Congress Cataloguing in Publication Data on p. 350

ISBN: 0-8281-3074-4 (regular) 0-8281-3073-6 (de luxe)
Book Trade Distribution by Simon and Schuster
A Division of Gulf & Western Corporation
New York, New York 10020
Ordering number: 13074 (regular) 13073 (de luxe)

Contents

Introduction   6

I   Settings   12

II   On the Move   34

III   Enterprisers, Great and Small   52

IV   Bad Moments   84

V   The Power and the Glory   98

VI   Rank and Station   126

VII   E Pluribus Not Quite Unum   148

VIII   Male and Female Created He Them   180

IX   Pandora's Box: The Stereoscope   200

X   Institutions   214

XI   Causes   250

XII   Lively Artists   268

XIII   On Stage   284

XIV   Simple Pleasures   306

XV   Epilogue: Glimpses of a New Era   330

Acknowledgments   350

Library of Congress Negative Numbers   350

Index   351

Introduction

By the 1890's the Library of Congress, still housed in the Capitol, was full to overflowing.

Just behind the Capitol, the Library appears under construction, to be completed in 1897.

The library (foreground) and annex today; to their right the library's Madison Building (not visible) is being finished and will one day be a home for the Prints and Photographs Division. At left, new display cabinets go up about 1903.

If one loves old photographs, with all their compelling magic, there is no happier a hunting ground than the Prints and Photographs Division of the Library of Congress. There, in the annex, known formally as the Thomas Jefferson Building, housed in long corridors of shelves, boxes, ancient green filing cabinets, and sometimes simply in piles, shedding and flaking at the corners, are the most variegated archives of old photographs in the world. Here are thousands of pictures by Mathew Brady and all the men who worked for him—daguerreotype portraits, Civil War coverage, postwar scenes—and the files of America's first news-photo agency, run by George Grantham Bain between 1898 and 1916, including up to one hundred twenty thousand glass-plate negatives as well as a smaller number of prints. Here are so-called "master prints" made by scores of famous photographers, and the first real war coverage, taken by the Englishman Roger Fenton in the Crimea. Then there are scenes of Czarist Russia, activities of early missionaries to Liberia, and portraits of long-dead professors at Harvard. If you enjoy personal albums, you can leaf through Clara Barton's, Alexander Graham Bell's, the Sultan of Turkey's, Josephus Daniels's, the Wright Brothers', and Hermann Goering's. If—but there is no end to it.

As to sheer size, the archives are probably the largest collection of photographs in the world. You have to say "probably" because all large libraries give only estimates of such holdings, and the Russians refuse to provide any figure at all. Even though the Library of Congress is one of the most efficient arms of American government, its photographic collection was gathered almost by accident. The guesses at the number of photographs, all provided by in-house experts, run anywhere from eight to fifteen million.

Naturally, there is an official figure, because government bureaucracies always require one. The last annual report of the Library of Congress, for the year 1976, lists "8,484,043 negatives, prints, and slides"—which is preposterous, because many large collections have never been opened, others are estimated, some are only partly processed, many include duplicates, and some, while not exactly lost, cannot be found.

What some of the photographs look like and what they tell us about ourselves and the America we left behind us is the subject of this book. But perhaps I should explain first how I got involved in this project.

Late in the 1950's when I was editing *American Heritage* magazine and very interested in unearthing fresh early pictures of the United States—ones never before used—I dropped in one summer day on the late Edgar Breitenbach, then chief of the Prints and Photographs Division. In the course of being most helpful Dr. Breitenbach took me to a large, steaming attic in the main building of the library. There, for lack of any other place,

7

were stored box after box, trunk after trunk, packing case after packing case of photographs—uncatalogued, unsorted, unknown. Dr. Breitenbach poked here and there into what struck his visitor as treasures; prying open one wooden box, for example, he found dozens of rolled-up panoramas, the long, wide photographs taken by a slowly turning camera. With it, large groups, landscapes, or cities were once recorded. It was depressingly clear to Dr. Breitenbach and to me that a great many rarities (and a great deal of trash) reposed in that attic, that he needed help to rescue them and sort them out, and that as things go with the Congress, money was not likely to be forthcoming. And it was not. Old photographs left lying in attics do not have much of a voting constituency.

Editors are busy, of course, and somehow for about twenty years I never returned to look further. Librarians are busy, too, but untiring Dr. Breitenbach before his retirement somehow did manage certain improvements. The packing cases and trunks are gone, and the pictures in the attic are now in an air-conditioned sub-basement in the annex, in cabinets or shelves. The majority of that Golconda has been sorted, after a fashion, mostly by the chief himself, with the help of devoted staff members. Some of the sorting is rather hasty—by size, for example, or by very general topics like "animals," or "navies" (any kind of navy). Indeed, some of the material has been catalogued, but new material pours into the library faster than a small staff can keep up with it.

Last year I did return to the Prints and Photographs Division and resumed the search contemplated so many years before. I was lucky to obtain the services of a first-class guide, Shirley L. Green, whose years of experience in the division and with archival photographs in general helped me pinpoint the unexplored areas and the lightly visited ones; she also knew which files would probably be less productive of new material —a great timesaver. The staff of the Prints and Photographs Division, as it always does, provided a great deal of help.

This book is the result of that exploration, which went on for many months, collecting thousands of photographs from which those shown here were, with considerable anguish, winnowed out—on the theory that a few pictures, reproduced in large size, speak more loudly than a great many little ones. They were chosen for rarity, or quality, for this is not in any way a history, but a sampling, however incomplete, of a notable and not fully appreciated national asset.

Strangely enough, there is not much of a literature on the holdings of Prints and Photographs, and what there is deals as well with the nonphotographic part of the archives—which, while much smaller in size, is nevertheless superb in its holdings of artists' prints, lithographs, posters, early advertising, cartoons, and drawings. The first printed catalogue, the *Guide to the Special Collections*, was compiled in 1955 by Paul Vanderbilt, then chief of the division. Though somewhat outdated and out of print, it is still the only one. *Viewpoints*, a book of handsomely illustrated selections, was issued in 1975 by Alan Fern, another ex-chief of the division, and Milton Kaplan, a former curator of nineteenth-century prints, but concentrates on the notable collections, in art as well as in photography. There exists no overview of the photographic archives alone.

Mathew B. Brady, who began his career in daguerreotypes, appears in one here with his wife, Julia, and his sister, Mrs. Hagerty. Much "Brady" work was actually done by his big staff.

Napoleon Sarony, his commanding head here superimposed on a tiny body, was a picturesque, popular portraitist of theatrical people.

Seneca Ray Stoddard, the great Adirondacks cameraman, took this shot of himself in 1870.

William H. Jackson began as a photographer of the West, managed the Detroit Photographic Company—and lived to be a hundred years old.

8

Dominated by its skylight, the studio of Frances Benjamin Johnston stands ready for action. By the 1890's this talented woman photographer was already famous for her documentaries.

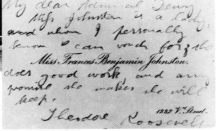

To help Miss Johnston, whose pictures of his own family he admired, President Roosevelt gave this enthusiastic card of introduction to Admiral Dewey. She wanted to cover him on his way back from his victory at Manila.

Lively and popular, Miss Johnston, left, and Gertrude Käsebier, another excellent woman photographer, pose in 1899 with photographers F. Holland Day, top left, Henry Troth, center, and Clarence White.

Lewis Hine, who spent most of his career propagandizing with his camera against child labor, appears as a shadow in this picture of a newsboy.

This is not to say that photographs from the Library of Congress are not used continually, indeed more every year, in countless books and magazines. In fact, some of them are used over and over again, until they have become clichés. The reading room of Prints and Photographs is usually full of visitors, and the mail with requests. What the researchers are looking through is not a single archive or catalogue but a collection of collections. Some of it—the most-called-for items, like the Brady material, or the presidential file, or the historic buildings survey—is readily accessible. A great deal more is kept in so-called "lots," or groups of pictures arranged by a photographer, a donor, or a subject,—all retrievable through a system of catalogue cards. There are almost twelve thousand lots, some of which are rarely consulted. Other large collections, like those of the Bain news service, have their own catalogues made by the original proprietors, not all of them very helpful. Some new accessions, like the giant morgue of the *World-Journal-Tribune*, roughly a million and a quarter pictures donated by that failed combination of venerable New York newspapers, are locked in a Maryland warehouse. There they and other valuables await the day when Prints and Photographs will move to fresh quarters in the new James Madison Building, still being completed across the street from the old main library building. Altogether the catalogued materials are estimated at about sixty percent of the holdings, however hard to get at some of them may be.

Why does so much remain unorganized and out of reach? Before criticizing, one would do well to reflect on a little history. The Library of Congress itself was founded originally with about a thousand dollars' worth of books that the early legislators needed for their work. They were ordered from London, only to go up in smoke in 1814 when the British burned the Capitol, and were replaced when Congress bought elderly Thomas Jefferson's own private collection of books. Thereafter, the library suffered two fires, one minor in 1825 and another that destroyed two-thirds of the collection in 1851. Although soon growing again, the library remained a modest affair until the advent in 1864 of Librarian Ainsworth Rand Spofford, an acquisitive collector who more than any other man transformed the institution from a modest service for congressmen to a great national library. By the time he retired in 1897, he had brought about the building of the original library building behind the Capitol.

But his greatest achievement, looking back over the years, came at the beginning of his tenure. He wanted, and got, the job of registering all copyrights in the United States. That was how he built the great collection of books—and all the other collections that went with it, including that of photographs. Before his copyright law was passed in 1870, photographs, like everything else, were deposited for copyright with federal district courts and thereafter carelessly handled. Many of the old photographs, if not lost along the way, were simply stuffed in bags. After a while they were sent to the State Department, which did not want them, and later to Interior, which stashed them in basements.

While a little of this material survives—very little—the main collection of photographs therefore really begins in 1870. Applicants sent in two prints of each picture, all too often marred on the front by scratched or painted-on lettering and rarely accompanied by adequate captions. Some, in fact, had none. And there were no negatives. In 1909 the flow of photographs for copyright dried into a trickle when another law made it possible to include photographs in the overall copyright of publications in which they appeared. In effect this new law took account of the invention of the halftone, which came into general use at the turn of the century.

Despite all these vicissitudes, the copyright collection, which is estimated to constitute about twenty percent of the archives, is a great, irreplaceable treasure. And one of the main parts of it is several hundred thousand stereographs, the double pictures on slides that give a three-dimensional effect when viewed through a stereoscope. The stereo companies, whose work goes back to the 1850's, concentrated on scenery, cities, travel, disasters, ordinary life, humor, and such news events as the building of the transcontinental railroad; without them much visual and social history would be lost.

What has swollen the photographic files of the library in the twentieth century has been transfers from other government departments—for example, the Farm Security Administration's collection of about 272,000 negatives and 150,000 prints of America in the years from 1935 to 1943; the bulging Office of War Information file; the thousands of captured German photographs taken in World War II; the thirty thousand photographs of the Historic American Buildings Survey, deposited by its sponsors, the National Park Service and the American Institute of Architects.

To this must be added such huge gifts as the *Look* magazine collection and that of the American Red Cross, some sixty-two thousand negatives and their accompanying prints of war and relief work; or the thirty thousand plates and twenty thousand prints of the Detroit Photographic (later "Publishing") Company. The last named, in which the noted western photographer William Henry Jackson was an active partner, was one of the greatest general publishers of photographs of almost every part of the United States. Some of these fine views (represented in this book) came in for copyright; others were donated. Gifts and bequests brought in valuable collections like that of the noted woman photographer Frances Benjamin Johnston; astute purchases accounted for such work as the photographs of Bain, Arnold Genthe, Fenton, and various Brady collections acquired in 1943 and 1944.

It is nevertheless only since World War II, with the growth of interest in history, preservation, and archival photographs themselves, that the true value of these collections has been widely perceived and much serious new work undertaken. Researching and cataloguing will extend into the next century, unless in a fit of madness the Congress were to increase the present corporal's guard that staffs the Prints and Photographs Division into a battalion. In that unlikely event, with every last picture neatly filed, catalogued, and cross-referenced, not to mention captioned, it is the author's view that the fun, so to speak, will be over, the thrill of discovery gone. Libraries exist to be dug into by scholars or amateurs, and in this case by what might be called pictorial private enterprise.

In this particular enterprise we have tried to sample the

The first big news-photo service, with some one hundred subscribing newspapers, was set up by George Grantham Bain, seen here at the wheel of his car, in front of his office on Union Square.

Camera clubs were a big thing in the early days, and this California group has naturally gravitated to a giant redwood, the General Sherman tree in the Mariposa Grove.

Looking at snapshots became a family pastime. Here Orville Wright (standing), his family, and some friends enjoy such an evening in Dayton. The Wright collection is now in the Library of Congress.

Selling photographs to tourists was a brisk business. At Fabyan's, New Hampshire, "View Artist" Peter Eddy shot the travelers taking the open cars to Mount Washington. When they got back from riding the connecting cog railway up the mountain they asked for their pictures by the number on the sign. The date of this picture is 1901.

The setup photograph became a popular genre, though not always with the young. The time is 1920, the photographer Herbert E. French, whose photo service covered Washington.

collections with unpublished or at least rare and forgotten pictures, hard as it is to be sure that some "unpublished" photograph may not in fact have been used by someone, somewhere. Unfortunately, no handy mysterious glow suffuses an old picture to indicate its virgin state, and one must fall back on those fallible old guides, memory and experience—plus indexes of known publications. In several cases, too, we have deliberately reproduced known photographs to make a point or to represent a collection or simply because we have never seen such a sharp original print of the subject. And no claims at all are made for the few pictures accompanying this introduction, some of which have been used many times before.

A few readers may find here pictures they recognize if only because copyrighted photographs were often widely sold at the time they were taken. Library of Congress pictures can be copied and even resold by commercial agencies unless subject to some restriction. But the very absence of a copy negative in the file— and also of an original negative—is at least some assurance that the picture is unused. So is a high number among the catalogued lots, indicating that the photograph has only recently emerged from the shadows. That is happening now, for example, to the large set of family, personal, and professional photographs of Alexander Graham Bell, donated by his heirs.

The period of this exploration is generally the years between 1870, when the copyright pictures started flowing into the library, and the 1920's, when, in my eyes, an era ends and the photographic record becomes massive and modern in appearance. Then in some indefinable way the unique flavor departs from the collections. Pushing and straining, historians can make "eras" out of almost any set of years that suits them, but there is nevertheless a genuine unity to the half century illustrated here. America, though still fundamentally rural, was on the verge of a new day—the age of expansion, the age of technology, the age of big business and small government. It was a time of formality, accepted inequality, and the usual human allotment of strife and trouble, but also of a great deal of unregulated happiness. It was the first half of the century that lies behind us—grandfather's and great-grandfather's day—far enough away to seem a strange country yet close enough at times to bring a tear to the eye.

In ways hard to put in words, photographs, especially the diamond-sharp images from the age of glass plates, have something that even great art lacks—a wonderful and terrible reality. Look at them under a magnifying glass, or printed large, as we have very deliberately presented them here. For all their odd hats, high collars, and impossible clothes, these generations, young or old but now dust, seem as young or old and alive as we ourselves. Here they are at work, posing with their achievements, working, playing, suffering, smiling at us, preserved as if it were not a century but an instant ago. To dig through the old boxes and turn the album pages, day after day in the library's stacks, is to pass through a ghostly door and begin to live among them. And coming out at closing time, past the guards and into bustling streets of the late twentieth century is like the shattering return of the time machine of H. G. Wells. Did it all happen? Did they all really exist?

Be comforted by the pictures.

I. Settings

America changes so fast that every few years a new crop of books is needed to describe the new face which things have put on, the new problems that have appeared, the new ideas germinating among her people, the new and unexpected developments for evil as well as for good of which her established institutions have been found capable.

—James Bryce

"Above, below, where'er the astonished eye/ Turns to behold, new opening wonders lie." Thus Edward Hicks, the primitive American painter, began the inscription above his picture of Niagara Falls in 1835. And in a similar mood, once cameras were up to it, photographers by the hundreds and then the thousands set out to record the settings in which the drama of America was laid. Here was the gorge, here the mountaintop; here were what the age called "noble prospects" of rivers, falls, plains, and cities. For the local cameraman there was Main Street, the courthouse and, with luck, the battlefield, where at the very least some patriot had received a glancing blow in the name of liberty. Besides that, there was industry to be served: factories, tourist attractions, new summer hotels, the railroad station. The camera was discovering America as it really was, and for the first time. It has to be realized that photographs were not yet a commonplace. The market for the commercial operative might be to furnish prints from which woodcut artists could fashion magazine or newspaper illustrations. But it was principally for stereographs, sets of three-dimensional pictures to be studied at home by a travel-hungry people. Later on, when the postal laws were changed, they would serve the penny-postcard industry. And the pictures poured in for copyright. Most of the photographs in this chapter, indeed in this book, happen to coincide in terms of dates with the experience in this country of James (later Lord) Bryce, the keen observer who is quoted at the left. The author of *The American Commonwealth*, the classic study of life in the late-nineteenth-century United States, traveled here widely seven times between 1870 and 1907, when he became British ambassador and stayed for six more years. The changes in his forty-three years of observation were great enough—the opening up of the West, the rise of industry and labor, the inpouring of new peoples, the growth of great cities. But the alterations in the purely physical, the "face which things have put on," in the half century since his death might strike Bryce today as bewildering and sometimes total. Anyone who has revisited his native heath after a long interval in these accelerated times will understand how the seemingly immutable scenes of childhood can be obliterated—and what indispensable aids to memory old photographs like these can be.

One of the first wonders of nature developed for American tourists was Ausable Chasm, a deep rocky gorge in the Adirondacks. Travelers came by Pullman and branch line to the head of the gorge and walked a path beneath the high walls, past marvels like Pulpit Rock and The Devil's Punch Bowl, to Table Rock. Here, in Seneca Ray Stoddard's photograph, the hardier types are going on for the thrilling boat ride to the foot of the rapids, all suitably dressed in their best clothes.

"Views" were highly esteemed by turn-of-the-century travelers, and in Baedeker's guidebooks they were rated with asterisks, one for fine and two for superb. Only one was allotted to Mount Tom, in Massachusetts, where these ladies in summer dresses and their attentive escorts are drinking in the winding Connecticut River and the haze-covered mill

town of Holyoke, then the biggest paper-manufacturing city in the world. Many self-respecting mountains like this, in tourist areas at least, had rack or cog railways to spare the viewers fatigue, and the neat platform and fencing recall a tidy age. This is one of a large collection of scenes made by the Detroit Photographic Company between 1898 and 1914.

Big trees were already rare in New England a century ago, but strong in associations, like the Washington Elm in Cambridge and the Charter Oak in Hartford. This one, on top of Sunset Hill, overlooking Squam Lake, New Hampshire, was the regular summer haunt of John Greenleaf Whittier, who loved to sit on the bench, where he wrote "The Wood Giant." One stanza

goes: "We saw our pine tree's mighty arms,/Above our heads extending,/We heard his needles' mystic rune/Now rising and now dying." There being more giant poets than giant trees in Whittier's New England, this one naturally became "The Whittier Pine" and was much revered by visitors. The quiet group here was photographed by D. W. Butterfield in 1887.

17

This somewhat brooding view of a proud but rather run-down southern planter's mansion—like so many in the Library of Congress collections—bears a terse and limited caption: "Washington's House, Mt. Vernon, Va., 1858. No neg." That was, of course, the very year in which the Mount Vernon Ladies' Association acquired the property from its last private owner, Colonel John Augustine Washington, in one of America's earliest and most successful ventures in historic preserva-

tion. Nothing could be done to refurbish the place until after the Civil War, in which both sides scrupulously avoided harming it. But afterward the balustrade above the main porch, and the little porch at left—later additions—were removed, and the missing column restored. The present archivist of Mount Vernon has what he thinks is the original negative but no identification of the white visitor. The black man seated at the corner may be West Ford, a freed slave who served as overseer.

Where the Buffalo Roamed

The herds of buffalo which gave this city its name were long gone when these fine views, with every sign on Main Street sharply delineated, were taken in 1870 by C. L. Pond. The classical First Presbyterian Church, at left below from street level, appears at right somewhat dwarfed and plain when photographed from scaffolding surrounding the tower of the new St. Paul's Church (see left foreground); by then the rage was for Gothic. Horsecars dominated broad avenues in a place where the first white man had put his dwelling place as recently as 1791. Burned by the British in 1812, buffeted by storms, Buffalo slumbered until the construction of the Erie Canal in 1825 made it the first gateway to the Great Lakes. Then the boom was on, only to be intensified when—at the time these pictures were made—the bustling harbor became the prize in the New York railroad wars of Cornelius Vanderbilt, Jim Fisk, and Daniel Drew. Through it poured lumber, grain, coal, and livestock. Buffalo made flour and beer and starch and iron and steel; it turned out railway cars and gave birth to the Otis Elevator Company. And presently St. Paul's had a new neighbor, the wonder of turn-of-the-century Buffalo, the Ellicott Square Building, which any native could tell you had sixteen elevators, serving a beehive of up to five thousand industrious souls!

Town & Country

Nothing pleases a photographer—or a viewer, for that matter—as much as something looking the way it is supposed to. The grimy but vital scene above, enlarged from an anonymous stereograph of 1903, is Pittsburgh in character. Smoke trails across the vast workings of the Homestead steel plant, sold just two years before by Andrew Carnegie to help create the huge United States Steel Corporation. Andy got $450 million and, meaning what he had always said about philanthropy, gleefully gave nearly all of it away. In 1892 Homestead

had been the scene of a pitched battle between its workmen and squads of Pinkertons brought in by the manager, Henry Clay Frick. Now in 1903 more progressive management, having discovered "labor relations," had excited the country with a huge profit-sharing scheme for workmen and bosses alike. If the fathers of the schoolboys above belonged to the lowest wage level, at some $800 a year, getting up $82.50 for a share of preferred was hard, but the payout in dividends, bonuses, and growth was spectacular for those who hung on.

Just as much in character as Pittsburgh but otherwise at an opposite pole is quiet, tree-shaded Main Street in Plymouth, New Hampshire, in 1908, where a child stares at the unusual spectacle of a photographer (from the Detroit Photographic Company again) at work in the middle of the road. Plymouth contributed buckskin gloves to the surging economy of the United States, but seemed little affected by the encroaching railroad at left. It was in this village that Daniel Webster had pleaded his first case, and here Nathaniel Hawthorne died.

23

Spring plowing in New England in 1899 was recorded in this moody photograph by G. E. Tingley of Mystic, Connecticut. Old-fashioned farming, with ox team and hand plow, still lingered in these narrow fields and stony pastures. But elsewhere, especially on the Plains, wonderful new machines had taken over. Cultivators, reapers, threshers, and like marvels

had increased production manyfold and made it possible for one man in 1890 to do the work of six or eight barely half a century earlier. Unfortunately for the farmers, this also meant lower prices and higher costs. Agitation spread—against the railroads, the gold standard, and the wicked East in general. Meanwhile, in droves, young men left their farms for the cities.

The Mall, principal promenade of Central Park in New York, had suffered neither elm blight nor crime blight in 1894, when this photograph was taken by J. S. Johnston, a little-known but able recorder of the metropolitan scene. Brigades of boulevardiers and their ladies saunter past uplifting statuary (Shakespeare, Burns, Columbus, *The Indian Hunter*), savoring

the delights of the great park designed *de novo* from swamp and slum in 1858. The silk hats and ladies' reticules were safe in that day, although in the slums crime of all kinds was rampant enough. The task of subduing it would be taken on the very next year, with great gusto but uncertain results, by a dynamic new president of the Police Board, Theodore Roosevelt.

Engines idling and ready to reverse for a smart landing, a steamboat glides up to idyllic French Point at Lake George, New York, in 1889. The thirty-three-mile-long lake, surrounded by mountains, was by then a noted summer resort, dotted with big summer hotels; but it had been the scene of war and massacre by the Indians during the French and Indian Wars. Celebrated in Fenimore Cooper's narratives for rugged adventure, its tame era is recorded by Seneca R. Stoddard's photographs, which cover the whole Adirondack range and adjoining areas in the 1880-1900 era. Stoddard also put out guidebooks and maps.

In the same year as Stoddard's photograph but a world away from placid Lake George, an unidentified man stands at the foot of Spearfish Falls, in the Black Hills of South Dakota. This great granitic outcropping is so well-watered and green, especially in contrast with the Bad Lands to the east, that Custer (invading the hills in 1874 in spite of a new treaty) wrote rather oddly that their beauty "may well bear comparison with the fairest portions of Central Park." This is one of a collection of photographs of the Dakotas, Wyoming, and Colorado by J. C. H. Grabill of Deadwood, South Dakota.

Call of the High Country

Out in the tall timber of the Cascade Mountains of Washington State a new society was growing up around Seattle and other Puget Sound cities as the century closed. The products of logging and mining went out; the visitors rolled in on the new railroads, and the gold dust sailed in from Alaska. It was rough and raucous country when Darius Kinsey reached it in the 1880's to ply his skills as a photographer, and ladies were a comparatively new phenomenon in the high country when he took the sightseeing party at the right on the slopes of Wilman's

Peak in the Cadet Mountains. At nearby Monte Cristo an attempt at silver mining by Rockefeller interests had just been wiped out by floods. The strange sight below, by H. E. Toles of Seattle, is one of the ice caves cut into the glistening green mass of Paradise Glacier on the south slopes of lofty Mount Rainier. By train on the Tacoma Eastern Railroad, then by stagecoach, and finally on foot to "The Camp of the Clouds," which rented tents and blankets, you made the trip in August or September and explored the many chambers of the glacier.

It is 1905, and somewhere along the tracks of the Chicago, Rock Island & Pacific a camerman named F. M. Steele is busy with an assignment from that far-flung road to record the wonders along its lines. Here is the large herd of some unidentified ranch, the owners, perhaps, posing with their rigs in the foreground. No doubt the squad of cowhands just behind them, who have obligingly roped and thrown an unoffending steer, wish the photographer would hurry with his work.

II. On the Move

How beautiful to think of lean, tough Yankee settlers, tough as guttapercha, with most occult unsubduable fire in their belly, steering over the Western Mountains to annihilate the jungle, and bring bacon and corn out of it for the Posterity of Adam.—There is no Myth of Athene or Herakles equal to this fact.

—Thomas Carlyle, in a letter to Emerson

Crowded in, eight, ten, and twelve abreast, the passengers in the big jets flash across America—five short hours from New York to California. Drowsy with cocktails and heavy meals, they doze or read or watch the movies. Even travelers by the little windows soon turn away, for what is there to see but a fluffy cloud bank or a kind of flat brown expanse, seven miles down, marked here and there by a river or a faint superhighway? Generations are growing up for whom this antiseptic experience is travel and for whom there are no famous trails, no mountain passes, no plains, no forests, no great railroads, nothing but a brief interval between identical-seeming airports, linked by identical freeways with identical cities. Down in the photographic crypt of the Library of Congress (and in many other collections, of course) lies the fading evidence of what it was like, a century or more ago, to move about the same vast spaces of the United States. In the early era of the first explorers, the prairie schooner, and the handcart, the record is limited mainly to the work of artists. The daguerreotype was not a handy outdoor instrument, and it required a long exposure; the wet plate, which came in during the 1850's, provides our best glimpse of wagon trains, of ships collecting within the Golden Gate, or surveyors in the West. It is the pictures of the transcontinental railroads, however, that give us the best idea of what the great open spaces were like. Pioneer photographers like A. J. Russell and A. A. Hart went along as the tracks of the Union Pacific pushed westward across the plains and the Rockies to meet the Central Pacific coming the other way from California. Their work, and that of Charles R. Savage, F. Jay Haynes, and William H. Jackson, is too well known to republish here. But there is much more to the travelers' record than that. As steel to a magnet, cameras in the late nineteenth and early twentieth centuries were drawn to anything that moved—and there was never a more exciting time in transportation history than that before the automobile and the airplane. The railroad, with its infinite variety in sizes, modes, and elegancies, went everywhere. Palace steamers met trains, quaint branch lines met majestic main lines, horse and electric railways served cities and suburbs, and here and there stage-coaches still performed their romantic office. The pictures in this chapter may give some inkling of wonders and excitements of travel that airline passengers will never know.

This photograph from the firm of Lawrence and Houseworth dates to 1866 and shows how one crossed the High Sierras in the days before the first transcontinental railroads joined their rails at Promontory, Utah, in 1869. The wagoners have had to cut their way through high drifts of lingering spring snow to get their teams moving along this road down from the crest of the Sierra Nevada.

On a wharf at Martha's Vineyard a paddle steamer delivers a new load of vacationers from the Massachusetts mainland. But it was the horsecar that caught the eye of the photographer, Dr. Willard Gibbs Van Name, who was not only associate curator of living invertebrates at the American Museum of Natural History but also an enthusiast determined to preserve the record of horsecars and other disappearing devices, which he recorded in many cities. Besides that, he was interested in early steam locomotives and the water wheels and other machinery of old sawmills and gristmills. Born in 1862, Dr. Van Name came of a brilliant New Haven, Connecticut, family; his father, Addison Van Name, was librarian of Yale for many years, and his uncle, a bachelor who lived with the Van Names, was the famous mathematical physicist Josiah Willard Gibbs. Dr. Van Name was also a conservationist before it was stylish; he fought encroachments on the national parks, and in those causes was a regular writer of outraged letters to the daily papers.

Somewhere in the Black Hills on their way to Deadwood, the Omaha Board of Trade pauses for a picture by Grabill, the pioneer photographer. The silk hats seem to betoken an outing, and one venerable sport on the leading stagecoach is giving a blast on his horn. Ho! for Deadwood, widest-open town in the Dakota Territory, full of saloons, soiled doves, and gambling hells. The gold strike here in late 1875 brought prospectors in the thousands, not to mention characters like Calamity Jane, Preacher Smith, and James Butler ("Wild Bill") Hickok, the quick-fingered law man who was credited with having killed twenty-seven men (he wouldn't talk about it himself). Having run out of gold, Deadwood struck silver and, finally, tourism.

The railroad locomotive, America's engine of destiny for well over a century, had a quality of drama as recognizable in its own times as in ours. Photography came along several decades too late to catch the puffings of the diminutive first wood burners. But there was still a toylike air to some of them in 1860, when the little jewel at left, a four-wheel switching engine, rolled out of the Rogers Locomotive Works in Paterson, New Jersey. Everything is natty, from the painting on the headlight to the engineer's top hat. She was built for the Nashville & Northwestern Railroad, and seized by federal troops in the Civil War. The most dramatic feat of the iron horse was to bridge the continent. Below is one of Alfred A. Hart's many stereographs of the construction of the Central Pacific Railroad, building eastward to join the westward-bound Union Pacific to complete the first transcontinental line in 1869. Like his more famous counterpart on the U.P., Andrew J. Russell, Hart sensed the many meanings of the great feat of linking the oceans by rail. Perhaps this individual Indian has been carefully posed in his sad, contemplative stance, but the picture speaks volumes.

Nothing is known about this fine photoprint of a sleeping-car interior in daytime. Its internal evidence suggests

the late 1880's—but only guesswork can identify the honeymoon couple, the missionary, and the runaway embezzler.

This busy, spotless scene from the height of the railroad age comes captioned simply "Railroad Station, Petoskey, Michigan." It is undated but looks to be about 1908 or 1910. Since Bruce Catton, *American Heritage*'s resident historian, lived there about that time—and recently wrote a personal history of Michigan called *Waiting for the Morning Train*—we sent him a print, calling special attention to the little boy who is standing in the crowd at right and obviously admiring the lordly engineer. It *could* be him, Mr. Catton replies, even to the Buster Brown collar and tie. "Certainly I was down there often enough," he goes on. "The picture shows the heart-of-the-city stations of the Pennsylvania Railroad, which in Michigan was universally known as the Grand Rapids and Indiana. . . . Everybody called it the GR&I, all sort of run together into one word. On the left is the regular passenger station, with Little Traverse Bay, an arm of Lake Michigan, dimly visible in the background. Northbound, the track led to Mackinaw City and the Upper Peninsula; south, to Grand Rapids, Chicago, Fort Wayne, Cincinnati, and God knows where. Especially in summer, this line carried a fairly solid through passenger traffic, complete with Pullmans, diners, and the like. Also in summer, it carried on a suburban traffic of amazing volume: so much so that they had to build this separate suburban station, with its overhead footbridge approach, at right (the station itself is out of the picture at the lower right). This traffic sent one-, two- and three-car open-platform trains up and down, all day long, from Harbor Springs to the northwest to Walloon Lake (Hemingway's town) to the south. All of these were 'resort towns,' full of summer hotels and cottages. I do not quite remember what the figure for daily arrivals and departures was, but as I recall it ran to about 80 per diem, suburban and long distance put together. The suburban station—tracks, overhead bridge, and all—has long since vanished; the main station still exists but has been cut up into gift shops; there has been no passenger service in or out for many a weary year."

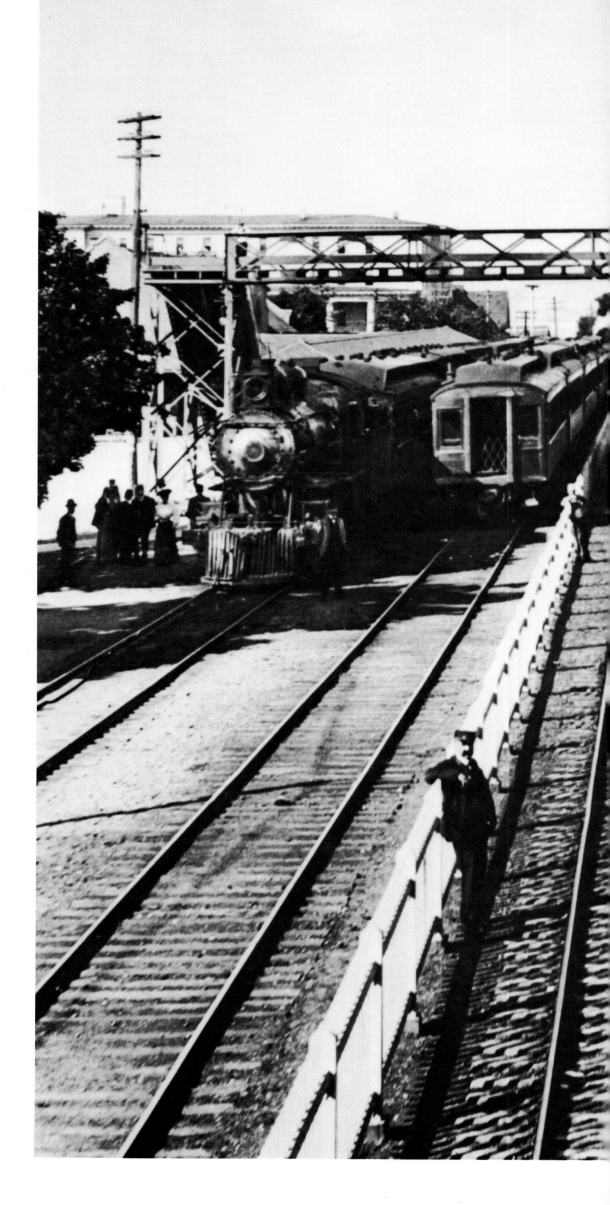

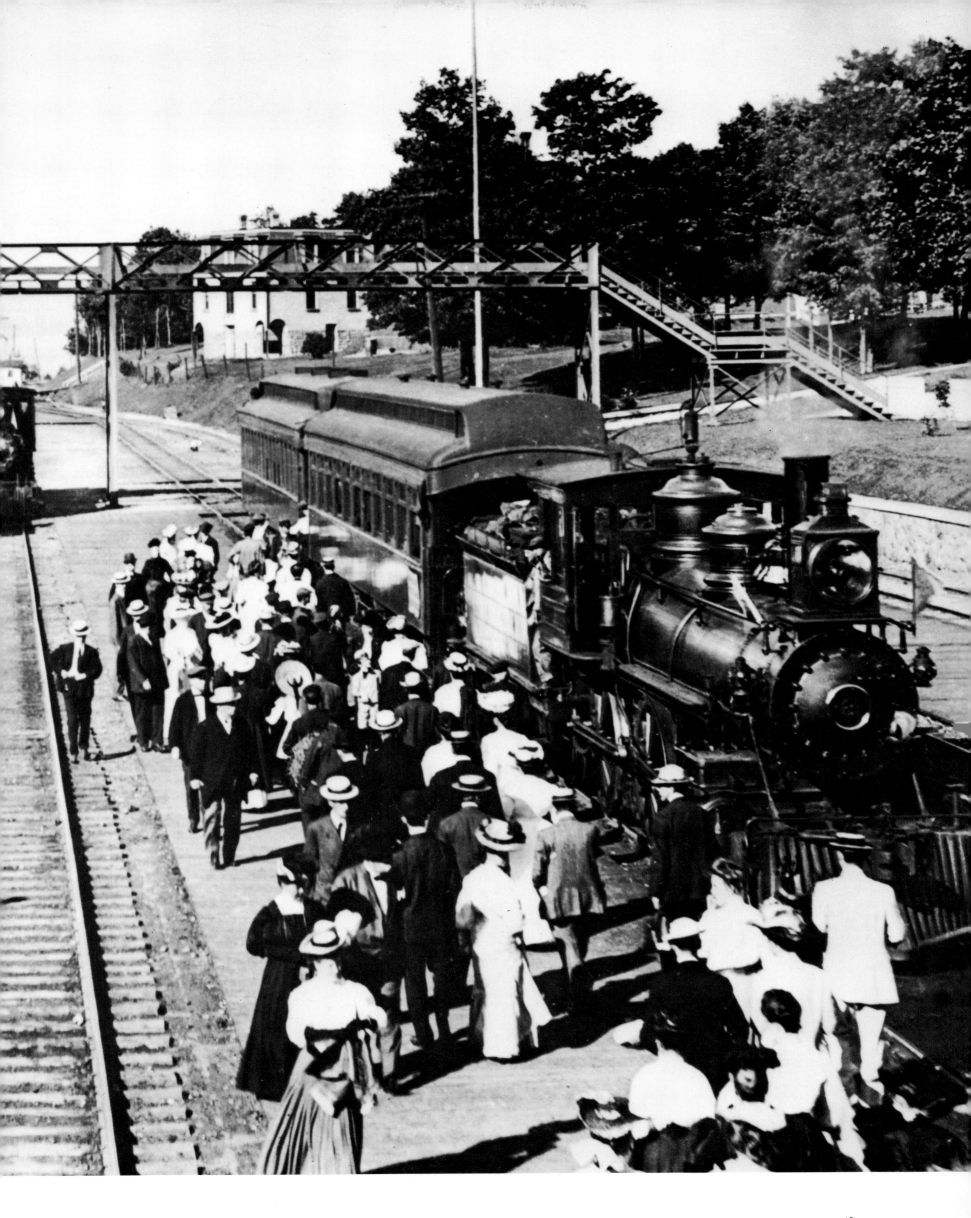

Rider Ed

The educational niche filled nowadays by "driver ed" was occupied in the early twentieth century—at least in this Brooklyn high school—by training in the art of boarding an open trolley car. This contraption, with wooden benches stretching the width of a car, had no center aisle but one or two long running boards. The rider stepped up, then slithered over anyone seated at the edge. The picture above shows the proper method, which involved waiting until the car stopped. But anyone of mature years will recall that the real fun was to jump aboard while the car was moving, linger on the step

while holding on with one carefree hand, then drop off again nimbly when the conductor inched up toward you in search of fares. The picture at the right, which also comes from George Grantham Bain's once popular news and feature service, exhibits a poor stance but inflammatory ankles, showing why the mashers at the soda fountain kept a sharp eye on the cars. It may be stated categorically that the open streetcar, dusting down boulevards and across meadows, blessed with nature's own free air conditioning, was the best form of local transportation ever devised by the hand of man.

The glory days of the river packets are recalled by this view of the Cincinnati levee; one of the last boats still plying the Ohio

and Mississippi, the *Delta Queen*, ties up here today. Behind is the Roebling bridge, a wonder of the age when completed in 1867.

Giant Step

These two photographs dramatize the giant steps taken by a nation on the move in a time of boisterous optimism and achievement. At the left, the battleship *Ohio* passes under tow through the Culebra Cut of the brand-new Panama Canal in 1915, part of a quiet, fifty-mile passage that took it through the waterway's six locks. Battleships like the two at right, laboring through steep Atlantic swells in 1911, three years before the first ship passed through the canal, had to steam an

additional seven thousand miles or more through such waters—and worse rounding Cape Horn—going from the east coast of the United States to San Francisco. The problems of digging the Big Ditch were enormous (there was the endlessly troublesome Cucaracha mud slide, for example, which may be glimpsed on the far shore). Yet the canal was built without graft, on time, and on budget, a monument to American initiative of the era—and a feat, alas, rarely repeated.

The Survivors

This collection of Old Testament faces belongs to the survivors of the first Mormon trek across the plains and mountains in 1847. "This is the place," said their leader, Brigham Young, as he looked around the arid valley of the Great Salt Lake and saw that it was good. And there, despite troubles with the Gentiles—which is to say, the rest of the United States—his people prospered and made the desert

bloom. There lingers about them, in this photograph taken fifty years after their great migration, an air of Moses and the ancient Israelites, or for that matter of the Voortrekkers of South Africa, who made a similar covered-wagon migration into their interior. The occasion for the picture was the 1897 Utah Pioneer Jubilee, and it was full of reminders of the turbulent Mormon past, from the murder of the first leader, Joseph Smith, to a quasi-Biblical plague of locusts, from which these children of the lost tribes were delivered by a dramatic incursion of seagulls. "The Holy City" was the song for the male voice contest. At the grand concert William Jennings Bryan, the perpetual candidate, was a guest of honor. There was a parade of floats, and fireworks, and for every one of the patriarchs and their durable womenfolk a gold medallion of Brigham Young.

III. Enterprisers, great and small

The close of the war with our resources unimpaired gives an elevation, a scope to the ideas of leading capitalists far higher than anything ever undertaken in this country before. They talk of millions as confidently as formerly of thousands.
—Senator John Sherman of Ohio to his brother, General William Tecumseh Sherman

There never was such a time in history to be not only a capitalist but also an enterpriser of any size whatever, an engineer, an adventurer, an inventor, a speculator, even a poor boy striving to make good in the manner set forth by Horatio Alger. The challenge of the Civil War had produced a tremendous response from business in the North. Afterward, if the South lay prostrate, the industrial revolution was in high gear in the rest of the country, and all this vitality and wealth were turned to expansion in every direction. The nation rang with the sounds of the builder's saw, the tracklayer's spike hammer, the miner's drill, the logger's ax. In what was sometimes outright exploitation with no thought of tomorrow, whole states like Michigan were denuded of their trees or overgrazed by cattlemen and overplanted by new settlers in the fertile plains. Iron, steel, textiles, paper, and oil had never enjoyed so many uses or experienced such spectacular growth. Cities exploded in size—downtown, in the slums, and along the streets of General Grant mansions built to the fussy Victorian taste of the new rich. There was never such a race to produce wealth, or one so uninhibited by government, or (for all its abuses) such a successful one. New inventions, astonishing if one had time to contemplate them at leisure, were soon accepted as normal—homes lit by electricity, workshops powered by it, the great distances linked by telegraph and telephone. Typewriters, sewing machines, farm machinery, high-speed presses, cheap watches, celluoid collars—what next? It was a sink-or-swim society, as we shall observe later, based on Herbert Spencer's economic interpretation of Darwin and "the survival of the fittest." The moral tone of this society depressed some aristocratic minds to the point that Henry James and Henry Adams, for example, spent long years abroad, but the average American, wedded to the behemoth of "progress," came to feel without realizing it that it would never end. The pictures of the era in the Library of Congress, which cover the long boom in a rich but haphazard way—depending on what photographers did or did not copyright—reflects its busy optimism. As a matter of course, wonders were expected from science and technology; automobiles, airplanes, moving pictures, even radio and television and the power of the atom were accepted as inevitable—so much so that to this very day many Americans cannot reconcile themselves to a world of limited possibilities and the fact that the party, unbelievably, seems to be over.

Proud of their jobs and in their natty best for photographer J. C. H. Grabill, the engineer corps of the Deadwood Central Railroad poses with its instruments and a good sample of rugged Dakota terrain one day in 1888. The railroad spelled finis for the stages seen in the last chapter, an unfortunate side effect of progress.

Washington was booming in the 1840's when this fine view of the new Patent Office was made; in this detail, private houses, their woodpiles, and other homely sights linger on to recall the small-town atmosphere. The scene is from a daguerreotype, one of six recently found in an Alameda flea market by a California collector and sold, after careful cleaning, at a nice profit to the Library of Congress. Others in the set show the Capitol with its small Bulfinch dome, the White House, and the General Post Office—unique treasures, because they are the earliest surviving photographic views of the city and are almost certainly the work of the early "daguerrian artist" John Plumbe Jr. At the right, and a continent away, workers

hold still for the cameraman on the brand-new ironclad monitor *Comanche*, about to be launched in 1864 at a San Francisco shipyard. The picture was one of a set issued by the western firm of George Lawrence and Thomas Houseworth, who also sold cutlery, optical equipment, and a "magneto-electric" machine supposed to relieve nervous diseases.

Sometime beween 1905 and 1910, when the uncaptioned picture at right was taken, American railroading was hitting its peak as the country's greatest industry, surpassing all others as a buyer of iron, steel, and coal, as a user of capital, and as the nation's largest employer (1,700,000 men in 1910). The rails dominated Wall Street interest; they carried almost everyone and every product, and in one way or another they would get you in or close to every town and almost every hamlet. The natty New Haven foreman at right had plenty of men in his yard crew, as did the shop below, producing huge locomotive wheels. The latter picture was taken by Waldron Fawcett in 1904. Railroaders were a proud, swashbuckling lot, yet they also tended to be fraternal and devoted to traditional ways. The public revered the "brave engineer," but met mainly the conductors, generally so commanding and austere a fraternity that many called them "Captain."

The figure of John D. Rockefeller was as awesome and enigmatic to his contemporaries as it remains to us today. He was always old, it seemed. The portrait is by Arnold Genthe (best known for his studies of the equally inscrutable Chinese of San Francisco). In it, is Mr. Rockefeller contemplating the perfect organization with which the Standard Oil trust has disposed of untidy competition? By 1878, the pious former bookkeeper controlled ninety per cent of the oil refineries in the United States. Is he baffled by his critics and the outcries of those whom they claim (quite foolishly, to his mind) he has "ruined"? Is he happy with the thought that the decline of the kerosene lamp has fitted in nicely with the rise of the automobile, thirsty for his gasoline? Is he pleased with the perfect lawn of his big Victorian house in Cleve-

The Ancient Colossus

The figure of John D. Rockefeller was as awesome and enigmatic to his contemporaries as it remains to us today. He was always old, it seemed. The portrait is by Arnold Genthe (best known for his studies of the equally inscrutable Chinese of San Francisco). In it, is Mr. Rockefeller contemplating the perfect organization with which the Standard Oil trust has disposed of untidy competition? By 1878, the pious former bookkeeper controlled ninety per cent of the oil refineries in the United States. Is he baffled by his critics and the outcries of those whom they claim (quite foolishly, to his mind) he has "ruined"? Is he happy with the thought that the decline of the kerosene lamp has fitted in nicely with the rise of the automobile, thirsty for his gasoline? Is he pleased with the perfect lawn of his big Victorian house in Cleve-

land, above? Or the day's take in the plate of the Euclid Avenue Baptist Church? Or the success of his empire of philanthropies, the greatest in history until his time? There are no sure answers. We do know that, having given away $530 million—some of it by passing out dimes—he grew to look more and more like Rameses II, the mummified pharaoh, and slipped away at 97, as incomprehensible as ever.

Lift up this page and the one opposite and fold them both outward to gain some idea of the vastness of the burgeoning American oil business over which Rockefeller presided. This extraordinary scene represents only one-third of a vast 360-degree panorama of the Long Beach, California, oil fields in 1923. Behind the beach and boardwalks the jungle of rigs pumped to satisfy the growing wants of the automotive age.

At the bottom of the free enterprise ladder, unconcerned with the battles of the goldbugs or the free silverites, probably unaware of even the names of Adam Smith and William Graham Sumner, a ragtag army of souls plied their trades. The ones below were captured by an unknown photographer in Chicago in 1891. It is doubtful if they could afford even the prices of the lunchroom opposite (taken, also anonymously, in St. Louis about 1900). Note that one of America's classic enterprises—Coca-Cola—has already made its appearance.

THE FLYPAPER AND MATCH SELLER

THE COALMAN

THE FEATHER-DUSTER MERCHANT

THE ITINERANT BILL POSTER

LOAF
2 c
OPEN
DAY
& NIGHT
1326
SANDWICHES LUNCHES
Fried Spring Chicken 10 & 15
Try Our ST. PAUL 10
Brains Scrambled with Eggs 10
HAM & EGGS 10
BOILED HAM 10
CHILE CON CARNE 10
HOT SPAGHETTI 5
Pan of Pork & Beans 5
HOT PIG FEET
Pickled Lamb Tongue
TURKEY
RABBIT 5
HAMBURGER
SPARE RIBS
WIENNIES
FALO FISH 5
CAT FISH 5
CROPPIE 5 & 10
JACK SALMON 5 & 10
SMELTS 5
SUN FISH 5
Pickled Herring 5
CAVIAR 10
Fish Ball 5
1326
DELICIOUS REFRESHING
Coca-Cola
5¢ IN BOTTLES 5¢
THE ST. LOUIS
ICE CREAM

To the steadily growing hum of industrial America, new enterprises brought new sounds—the subterranean picking in mines, the roar of smelters, the crash of steel mills, the slapping of leather belts. At right, working off a central shaft, hundreds of belts power the machinery at the National Cash Register Company, recorded by a Detroit Photographic Company man in 1902. Water power for such mills had long since yielded to steam, which in many cases would soon be replaced by electricity as the prime mover in thousands of settings like this. About the scene below we know only that these are silver miners and that the time, in the smudged copyright notice, seems to read 1892. Mining was the physical bottom of enterprise, but the hard work was balanced by the faint possibility that you yourself might find a Comstock Lode. Mining lay behind the legendary "Haw" Tabor of Virginia City, produced folk figures like "the unsinkable Molly Brown," and gave a start in life to one President, Herbert Hoover, who worked in a mine as a youth ten hours a night, every night of the week, for two dollars per day. The fortunes, he soon perceived, would be made in engineering, not by chipping away at the earth—just as provisioning, not panning in a cold mountain stream, had paid off in the gold fields of '49.

Anything big was irresistible to Americans—trees, for example. With the eastern forests stripped, Yankee loggers went west to clean out Michigan, where the somewhat unbelievable scene at right was caught by G. A. Werner in 1893. This special load of logs, containing 36,005 board feet of timber, was hauled out of the woods by *one team of horses* for exhibit at the World's Columbian Exposition in Chicago later that year. Other loggers working the sequoia groves of the Pacific coast found their photographer in the person of Darius Kinsey; he was a small man who made big trees his life-long interest. "You aren't a logger," he would say, "until you have your picture taken with a tree." This homely scene, less spectacular than most of his work, shows a tree he calculated by the rings to be one hundred twenty-nine years older than Methuselah, and he found a suitable old man to lean on it. But as sequoias go this was a mere sapling.

Curb & Sill

The center of finance for the new industrial colossus was Wall Street and the maze of old Dutch cow paths around it. This fine, crowded scene, extracted from a 1902 panorama by B. J. Falk, looks up Broad Street from Exchange Place to Wall Street. In the foreground is the picturesque confusion of the old Curb Exchange. Here, rain or shine, even in blizzards, met the curbstone brokers and, until the coming of the telephone, the runners who carried their orders back and forth to offices. Even after phones were installed, clerks like the boy above perched on window ledges and other vantage points to relay orders between phone operators and brokers, either by shouting them or using a system of hand signals. Brokers were supposedly honor-bound not to read rival signals, or at least not to act on them. The Curb men dealt in the securities not listed on the main exchange, making up in noise and color what the companies they traded lacked in quality. Finally, in 1921, they too moved indoors, and then in 1953 became the dignified American Stock Exchange. In the middle of the street there is a glimpse of a Dow Jones & Company delivery wagon with a load of *Wall Street Journals*.

Ever-improving transportation helped make cities grow in the booming years after the Civil War; the radius within which ordinary people could handily get to business was lengthened by the horsecar and the trolley, then vastly increased by rapid transit. On Manhattan's West Side the steam-operated elevated railroad built to the north faster than the speculators and house-builders could follow it, as demonstrated at the left in a curious 1883 photograph by Charles Pollock of Boston. The scene is "Angel's Curve" (so high that one could "hear the angels sing"), where the Ninth Avenue line, after turning east on 110th Street, swung north on Eighth Avenue into the middle-class rural village of Harlem. Nothing but a goat cart and someone's fence indicates human habitation. But by 1886 the New York *Times* was exulting over the rows of houses and apartments that had sprung up, and the fact that the rock outcroppings, goats, and shanties had vanished. Subway construction, which came later, was a very different matter. The scene below at Union Square shows how the work had to be done, at much greater expense, while the busy traffic of surface cars was uninterrupted. Most of the Els were torn down in the 1930's, although the Third Avenue line lingered on until 1955. Many of improvident New York's traffic woes are a consequence of demolishing these useful services without providing alternative subways first.

These gentlemen have just arrived at the office, but they are all ready to process your land claim, bring a lawsuit, or (if you will wait a few hours) rent you a room. Their clients and fellow townsmen, as the wagons and buckboards indicate, have just arrived too, and the most pressing question is where to put Main Street—and the saloon. We are at one of the feverish land rushes in which former Indian lands were opened by Congress to settlers—or simply seized by boomers. The indistinct caption seems to read "1889" and indicates almost certainly that this is the so-called Oklahoma District land rush of that year, when Oklahoma City, bare prairie at noon, had gained a population of ten thousand by nightfall.

The United States took over the Panama Canal Zone and the old French diggings in the same rough-and-ready way it opened the West, but there the resemblance ceased. The cleanup and the building were handled with great order and good sense by both John Stevens and his successor in charge, Colonel G. W. Goethals. The toughest job was the nine miles of the Culebra Cut, a mountain-moving task that dwarfed any single engineering achievement in previous history. This picture shows a little part of it in progress in 1907. Despite rain, mud, and slides, six thousand men, fifty to sixty steam shovels, and three hundred rock drills chewed away daily at Culebra until the first ocean-going ship, a cement boat named *Cristobal*, passed through the whole canal on August 3, 1914—almost unnoticed because on that day Europe was beginning the First World War. Goethals, who was paid fifteen thousand dollars a year to build the canal, was offered the new position of governor of it, at a salary which the ever-grateful United States Senate later reduced to ten thousand.

He had invented, it would seem, just about everything: electric lights and then the magical phonograph, with the little cylindrical records that let you hear William Jennings Bryan and Harry Lauder and "In the Good Old Summertime." On the musical records a voice announced the title before the band started, and added, "played by the Edi*sone* Military Band." The great man was deaf and liked to have words clearly, if strangely, stressed: "Edi*sone*," "rec-*kord*"—accent the last syllable. He gave us motion pictures, founded utilities, and experimented with everything. Below, he shows off a model of a proposed low-cost cement house, and at right, at his New Jersey estate, he takes his youngest son, Theodore, for a spin in an Edison electric car. Whenever he tired of the laboratory he would go camping with friends like Henry Ford and John Burroughs. His whole approach to life, said Edison's wife, was "to shove more than sixty minutes into an hour."

Curtiss & Wright

Samuel Pierpont Langley was not only a well-known astronomer who had explored the infrared parts of the solar spectrum but the elderly and dignified Secretary of the great Smithsonian Institution. Various experiments, and consultations with the noted Dr. Alexander Graham Bell (then working with kites), convinced him that heavier-than-air flight was possible, given sufficient velocity. In 1896, with a steam-powered pilotless model he called an "aerodrome," weighing twenty-six pounds and looking somewhat like a miniature of the device below, he managed a successful flight of about three-quarters of a mile (which was all the distance his fuel and water would last). But when in 1903 he attempted to launch a man-carrying version, exactly like the one below, it crashed ignominiously in the Potomac. The ridicule of the press crushed Langley and cut off his congressional source of funds. But in 1914 Glenn Curtiss reconstructed Langley's plane from the original plans, tinkered a little, and made the successful flight shown in this picture from the Grosvenor-Bell Collection. Dr. Bell was his sponsor.

The newspapers, having broken the spirit of Professor Langley, generally ignored or simply published as a brief unproved assertion the news that the Wright Brothers had actually made the first powered airplane flight in history on December 17, 1903. The editors were not going to be made fools of again. The War Department, as might have been expected, was not interested and would not bother with an inspection. It was in Europe, in 1905, especially at French air meets, that brother Wilbur astonished the primitive world of flying with the accomplishments and maneuverability of a newer Wright plane. At home it was Orville, shown above taking his sister Katherine for a ride in a later model, the HS of 1915, who continued the work until recognition first came, around 1908, from the Army. The Wrights' triumph was tragically marred by Wilbur's death from typhoid in 1912 and by a long, unpleasant patent fight with Glenn Curtiss, whom they looked down on as little more than a stunt man. Curtiss, known as "the fastest man on earth" for his motorcycle speed records, had been sought out by Bell during his search for a way to power his giant kites. Although the final result of the legal struggle was a jointly patented "Curtiss-Wright" engine, the feud between Wilbur and Curtiss was never ended.

By 1907 the invention of the telephone was thirty years behind him, but Alexander Graham Bell was busier than ever with new devices in many fields. On the opposite page, the leonine old man is demonstrating the use of his tetrahedral cells, so strong that four men could stand on a section (below) and so light that from them could be erected an eighty-foot observation tower without scaffolding or derricks—or even any climbing. Out of his tetrahedrons he built kites, then went on into aviation with Glenn Curtiss and other young disciples, whom he organized into the "Aerial Experiment Association." Bell had been president of the National Geographic Society from 1896 to 1904, and his daughter Elsie had married Gilbert H. Grosvenor, of the family that still manages the society today. All the Bell pictures here are from a large family collection recently donated to the Library of Congress by the Grosvenors. It is a superb source for one of the most brilliant and attractive figures in our history. If he had done nothing else, Bell would have been famous for his work with the deaf. Among his many students were his wife Mabel and a deaf, dumb, and blind girl of six named Helen Keller, whose father brought her to Bell in despair. For her, Bell and the miracle-working Annie Sullivan opened the door to life.

Sturdy old Bell leans forward intently one day in 1919 as a record-breaking hydrofoil speeds toward him on a Nova Scotia lake at 71.8 miles per hour. The machine had been designed and built by Bell and one of his many protégés, F. W. ("Casey") Baldwin. The picture was taken by his son-in-law, Gilbert Grosvenor, and perfectly captures the ag-

ing inventor's perpetual eagerness of spirit. He poured out the money he made from the telephone patents to students, young inventors, and his friends the deaf until he died in 1922 and was buried in Nova Scotia at his home, Beinn Bhreagh, on a hilltop overlooking the sea—while for a few moments all the telephones in North America were stilled.

IV. Bad Moments

I was only six years old then but I remember now that it seemed as if we were in a bowl looking up toward the level of the sea and as we stood there in the sandy street, my mother and I, I wanted to take my mother's hand and hurry her away. I felt as if the sea was going to break over the edge of the bowl and come pouring down upon us.

—King Vidor, the film director, recalling the Galveston hurricane

As old theatrical masks remind us, tragedy is the other side of comedy, sometimes a mere hairsbreadth away. A man falling from a high window is a ghastly spectacle until, as will happen, his suspenders catch on a flagpole and save him. Suddenly the event becomes ludicrous. In similar fashion George Bernard Shaw transformed a terrified Christian, thrown to the lions in a Roman amphitheater, into Androcles, the lion's friend. It is not too difficult to turn gasps into guffaws. Consider now the frame house at left. On September 8, 1900, the bustling, growing city of Galveston, Texas, was hit by a tremendous hurricane, with winds raging up to one hundred ten miles per hour. Galveston stood on a low island, nowhere more than a fraction over eight feet above sea level. Washing over it in fury, the storm left a mound of twisted, battered buildings, wiped out fifteen hundred acres of city entirely, and left six thousand to eight thousand dead; there could be no precise figures. Along with relief workers and Clara Barton herself, leading the Red Cross, photographers poured in. Their greatest pictures, or many of them at least, have about them some of that same close relationship of horror and humor. It is the bizarre that arrests us the most. "House on Avenue N slightly moved by flood," reads the original caption. Slightly! But it was not the photographer's own house. Another Galveston picture, on the next page, of a canted schoolroom, has a similar air to it; both are from a box of home stereoscopic slides on the disaster, sold all over an eager world by the alert firm of Griffith & Griffith. The call of calamity is strong, and the late Victorian Age provided it in plenty. Bigger ships, higher but often rickety bridges, faster trains on uncertain roadbeds—all made their contributions. And disaster, out of some curious perversity still within us, was box office. You could turn it into theater, or even stage a disaster, as the last few pages of this chapter demonstrate.

The disasters that are brought into your living room today by Walter Cronkite—various good camera angles on the correspondent at the scene, a few split-second shots of something smoking in the distance —are feeble fare compared with the old-time disaster coverage of the stereoscope. That was muscular stuff: hundreds of slides, real victims, horrifying details—and all in the third dimension. The slide opposite, showing Galveston hurricane ruins, is a good example. If a disaster was near your home, you forgot the stereoscope and took a special excursion train like the one at right to see the ruins. The roundhouse at Boulder, Colorado, has burned, and the sensible railroad company is recovering a little of its lost money from the curious.

For all their horror, natural disasters have their freakish side—the boat deposited on the railway tracks as if ready to start off, the meal undisturbed on the dining room table when the wall has been torn away. Thus, below, these locomotives in the East St. Louis, Illinois, roundhouse of the Baltimore & Ohio Railroad seem oddly unscathed after a great tornado in 1896. The picture was taken by William Schiller. At the left, the desks of a schoolroom, all screwed to the floor in the usual neat rows, lend a note of slanted decorum to a scene after the fearsome Galveston hurricane. This stereograph shows the school at Twenty-fifth Street and Avenue P; it was made by a visitor from Niagara Falls named M. H. Zahner. Many of those lost in the hurricane had sat at these little desks; no previous American storm had ever taken such a toll.

A fire wagon, below, was one of many employed in the grisly task of hauling away the dead in the Galveston disaster. The picture is by W. A. Green, otherwise unidentified. Weeks, and in some cases months, were required to find thousands of victims, many buried in debris, others lying under houses that had floated about the streets at the height of the storm. Because of the danger of epidemic, the bodies were loaded on ships, taken out to sea, and consigned to the deep. Insufficiently weighted, many drifted back ashore to add to the horror. In time Galveston recovered, raised its ground level, and built a great seventeen-foot sea wall.

Fires struck America's big cities in the late nineteenth and early twentieth centuries with a violence hard for later generations to comprehend, partly because the cities were a mass of hazards, partly because fire-fighting methods had not kept up with growth. On February 7, 1904, fire raging out of control wiped out the business district of Baltimore. Not even dynamiting saved the tinderbox office buildings; but by good fortune the blaze erupted on Sunday when businesses were closed, and no lives were lost. As one studies William H. Rau's photograph of blackened ruins, one remembers similar scenes in Chicago, Boston, and New York.

It was March 4, 1897, the day of the McKinley inauguration in Washington, a busy day as usual at the bustling corner of Tremont Street (foreground) and Boylston Street in Boston. The crossing was thronged with people, carriages, horsecars, and the electric trolleys that were slowly superseding them (although both could use the tracks of the electrified lines). The intersection was covered with planks, beneath which the new Boston subway lines were being constructed. And there was a maze of gas and water mains, which had to be moved about; indeed, there had been complaints of a strong smell of gas earlier that day, spreading over the Common and noticeable as far away as Park Street Church. Suddenly, when three streetcars were crossing or turning, the gas let go with a roar. The planking rose, and with it one streetcar and the horses of the next behind it shot into the air. Two other cars were lifted a little less, and the streets were showered with glass. In two or three cars, passengers were blown out of windows, and two cars burst into flames. People were seen trying to claw their way out. In the wreckage shown here, it is possible to spot the metal cowling of the end of one car and the battered state of another horsecar in the foreground. The electric car next to it seems undamaged. Two streetcar men were killed outright, and scores of people were hurt. The coupé of the Misses Bates of Boston went over, killing Miss Amelia Bates and their coachman. A cab, its driver, its passenger, and its horse met their ends together. Boston photographer Elmer Chickering got there in time for this gripping picture of the aftermath.

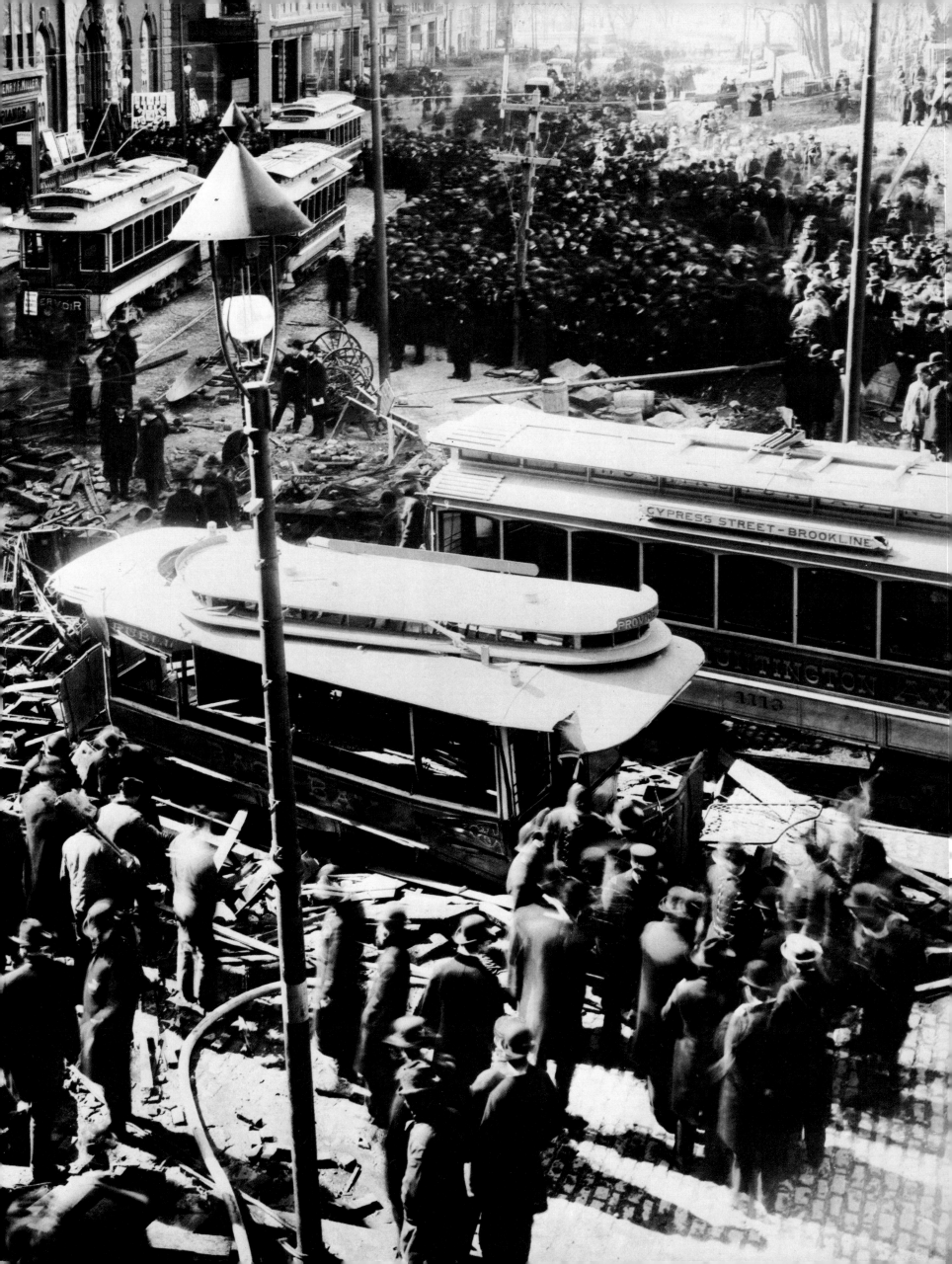

Dayton, Ohio, was the home of the Wright Brothers, who lifted man into the air, but when the Miami River overflowed in March, 1913, rescuers fell back on such ancient means as the old scow above to lift an elderly couple to safety. Man and wife are displaying great dignity, paying no attention to the man from George Grantham Bain's photographic service, apparently only a few feet away. Much less aplomb character-

izes the Model T Ford at the right, which in some unrecorded manner has come to rest half on and half off a streetcar boarding platform in Washington, D.C., its front wheels wearily splayed apart like a partly peeled banana. No one seems to care in the slightest or take any notice except the alert cameraman from the National Photo Service. Could that be the driver, heading off to continue his journey by trolley?

Disaster Revisited

From an entrepreneurial point of view, a disaster was a frustrating thing: it was impossible to predict when or where a real crowd-pleaser would occur. The problem was solved at the great amusement resort of Coney Island with the creation of spectacles that ran in theaters like these. Re-created chaos paid well; in 1903, when William H. Jackson took these views for the Detroit Photographic Company, all three of these houses were operating profitably within a mile of each other on Surf Avenue, Coney's main drag. The productions, forerunners of our current plague of disaster movies, were elaborately staged, with intricate sound and lighting effects and much vivid destruction. For only twenty-five cents, visitors to the Galveston Flood building saw the total demolition of a complex model of the entire harbor city. The producers kept up with the latest in catastrophes; when, for instance, an earthquake destroyed Messina in 1908, the Johnstown Flood—which had stopped pulling in customers—became The Great Italian Earthquake. The producers also understood that the public preferred to enjoy its carnage in total safety—as one selling point for its show, the producers of the Mont Pelée disaster made clear that their twelve-hundred-seat theater was well provided with exits and could be emptied in two minutes. It is a pity that the island of Martinique itself was not so thoughtfully equipped.

Watching restaged models of disasters in theaters was one thing, but how much better to put on the real thing itself! Railroad wrecks, for instance. On many occasions old steam locomotives would be smashed together for paying spectators, the crews setting the throttles and then jumping off. This 1896 "crash" crowd was photographed by H. F. Pierson of Denver. Another big head-on bang in 1896, put on by a man aptly named W. G. Crush before thirty thousand Texans in Waco, got out of hand. Flying scraps of boiler killed one spectator and badly hurt two photographers.

V. The Power and the Glory

Since the heroes of the Revolution died out
. . . some sixty years ago, no person
except General Grant has reached the chair
whose name would have been remembered
had he not been President, and no President
except Abraham Lincoln has displayed
rare or striking qualities in the chair.
—James Bryce, *The American Commonwealth*

The famous book cited in the epigraph at left was published in the same year, 1888, that the gentleman in the picture opposite was elected to the supposedly powerful and glorious office of President of the United States. And the title of the chapter in which Bryce made this observation, "Why Great Men Are Not Chosen Presidents," fully fits the occasion. Benjamin Harrison, honest, "safe," noted mainly as the grandson of "Old Tippecanoe," President William Henry Harrison, was another nonentity in a long dreary row between the Civil War and the end of the nineteenth century. Politics in far-off Washington seemed to most Americans a shabby business, unlikely to call great men to office. Indeed, in the administrations of Andrew Johnson and U. S. Grant, the so-called Radical Republican Congress fairly usurped the executive power. Then, in 1876, an election was actually stolen in the Electoral College, placing the otherwise upright Rutherford B. Hayes, a Republican, in the White House in a shady bargain with the South. In return for a few disputed electoral votes in occupied southern states, the Republican party agreed to withdraw federal troops, in effect restoring the former rulers to power. The cause of racial equality was thereby set back for the better part of another century. In general, the real issues of the time—deflation, financial panics, labor trouble, agricultural unrest, the abuses of the trusts—were never addressed in any effective way. Economics, everyone except the Populists believed, was not the true province of government, which degenerated into a scramble for office. The real power and glory in the Gilded Age belonged to the steel masters, the great bankers, the successful inventors of new industries, and, as Bryce himself emphasized, the presidents of the great railroads, whose movements about the country were like a royal progress. Which is not to say that the personalities and adventures of the gray, forgotten presidents did not interest newspaper readers. They hung on the impeachment of Johnson and the Grant scandals. Morbid sentimentality surrounded the slow death of James A. Garfield, shot down by an office seeker. Millions applauded, or laughed at, the temperate ways of "Lemonade Lucy" Hayes and the marriage of plump, forty-nine-year-old Grover Cleveland to a twenty-two-year-old college girl. But it was as hard for the photographers of the age as it was for the public to get very absorbed in these plodding chief executives until a new century dawned and another assassin's shot gave them Theodore Roosevelt, real presidential power, and what America secretly loves—a big, rollicking royal family in the White House.

The umbrellas of the dignitaries and the lack of them for the lesser folk below make a notable photograph of the inauguration of Benjamin Harrison on March 4, 1889. He stands at the left, bareheaded, while Chief Justice Melville W. Fuller administers the oath.

His Superfluous Excellency

Even among the well-informed, very few today can recall Garret Augustus Hobart. But if the anarchist assassin Leon Czolgosz had killed William McKinley in his first term rather than his second, the gentleman in this picture and not Theodore Roosevelt would have gone to the White House. Speculation is no doubt idle, although Vice-Presidents must secretly indulge in it. (One once observed that his main job was to get up in the morning, check on the President's health and, if the report was good, go back to bed.) Hobart was a New Jersey politician, a lawyer who specialized in receiverships and was at one time connected with sixty corporations. Here he poses just after his nomination with his family on the porch of his Paterson, New Jersey, estate, Carroll Hall, amid congratulatory floral offerings of the type associated in later times with the obsequies of gangsters. While he was in office, Hobart's best-remembered contribution to statecraft was his casting of the deciding vote in the Senate against the bill to grant independence to the Philippines. He was a gold supporter, and his most notable remark was in his acceptance speech. Referring to the free-silver question, he said, "An honest dollar, worth one hundred cents everywhere, cannot be coined out of fifty-three cents of silver plus a legislative fiat." It is, on reflection, an interesting thought, even in the late 1970's.

Republican Princesses

"Isn't this picture pure rapture? What an incredible dress; it had a sort of bib in front. I know that I must look as funny here as some of you will if you stay around as long as I have. You seldom get as good a laugh as when you are looking at old photographs of yourself." These are recent comments of Mrs. Alice Roosevelt Longworth, ninety-four at this writing, to the authors of *A Talent for Detail,* a biography of Frances Benjamin Johnston, who took the portrait in the White House conservatory. It was a little more than a year after the assassination of President McKinley. When the news of the shooting reached seventeen-year-old Alice, with its portent for her father if the President should succumb, she recalled for another recent interviewer that "my brother, Ted, and I danced a little war dance. Shameful! Then we put on long faces." Alice Roosevelt was one of the brightest attractions of the lively White House in Theodore Roosevelt's time. She was beautiful, daring, and clever; she smoked cigarettes in public, drove a car—which was novel enough—and, naturally, went too fast. The author Owen Wister once asked his friend, her father, if he couldn't control his eldest daughter. "I can either run the country or control Alice," said T.R., "not both." The young beauty went on to marry a congressman who became speaker of the House, Nicholas Longworth, and has been an outspoken fixture of Washington life ever since.

Pretty Frances Folsom was twenty-one when she married President Grover Cleveland, forty-nine, in 1886, the year the photograph at right was taken. He had been "Uncle Cleve," her guardian since the death of her father, but a visit to the White House, supposedly to the bachelor President's spinster sister, launched a slow-moving, highly proper romance. After a honeymoon marred by a prying press, which even followed them with spyglasses, Mrs. Cleveland proved a highly popular First Lady and the rejuvenator of her corpulent and somewhat lethargic husband.

When Harrison temporarily ousted Cleveland from the presidency in 1889, the former Caroline Lavinia Scott became First Lady. In the picture below, taken by "G. Parker" that year, we have the more standard occupant of that position. She fitted her overstuffed and heavily formal era, and reminds us of a few lines from William Allen Butler's once-famous *Nothing to Wear:*
Dresses for breakfasts, and dinners, and balls;
Dresses to sit in, and stand in, and walk in;
Dresses to dance in, and flirt in, and talk in;
Dresses in which to do nothing at all;
Dresses for Winter, Spring, Summer and Fall;
All of them different in color and shape,
Silk, muslin and lace, velvet, satin and crape.

In 1892 Mrs. Harrison died and her husband was defeated. Harrison later solaced himself by marrying his wife's niece, but the Clevelands were back in the White House. Times were difficult, what with financial panic and farm and labor troubles, and White House life was restrained. Mrs. Cleveland already had two children by the time the group opposite was posed by C. M. Bell of Washington in 1894. Around her are ranged the ladies of the Cabinet. Eight years since the picture on the preceding page had plumped her up somewhat, but she kept enough charm to make a second marriage five years after Cleveland's death in 1908.

Namesakes

The twenty-third President, Benjamin Harrison, was not blessed with popularity or a winning personality. He defeated Grover Cleveland narrowly in 1888, winning the electoral but losing the popular vote, and Cleveland ousted him easily in 1892. Harrison was an aloof Presbyterian elder, of whom a boyhood friend from Indiana once remarked, "I do not think he ever had an acquaintance with anyone that ripened into the hottest kind of friendship." Just the same, President Harrison received that one very American form of adulation which comes at the baptismal font: strangers' children were named for him. Nothing to match Washington or Lincoln, of course, or even Henry Clay (who never got elected), but—as the Library of Congress archives reveal in a neglected corner—Harrison treasured the few he got. A little file from the Harrison papers, "Lot 5313," disgorged the cabinet photographs on these two pages, sent to him by parents who had named their offspring for him in one way or another—sometimes including his Vice-President, Levi P. Morton of New York. We show about half of the file, beginning at left with Benjamin ("Jemy") French Schulze of Kansas, twenty months, gotten up by his parents as a farm boy.

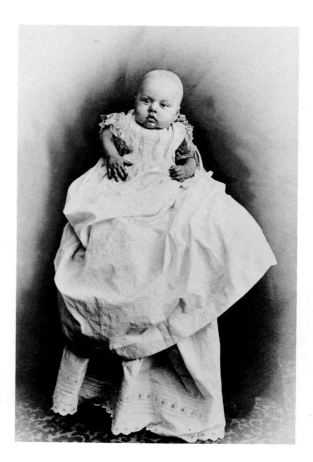

Benjamin Harrison Williams was photographed in Jacksonville, Illinois, by self-styled "XPERT FOTOGRAFER" McDougall.

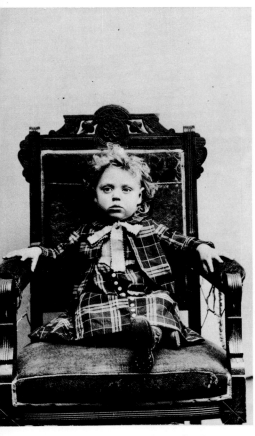

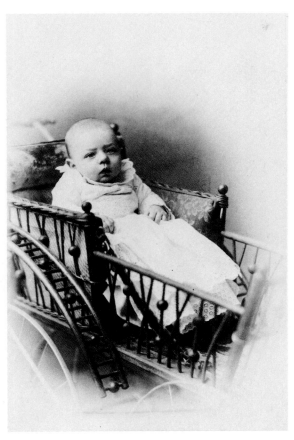

This wee Scot is described on the photograph as "Benjamin Harrison, son of George Parcy, Peru, Ind."

Benjamin Harrison Chase was born in 1892 in Los Angeles, California, to a railroad engineer who already had another son aged 53.

Benjamin Harrison Huffman sits with his brother Levy [sic] Morton Huffman; the boys lived in Elizabethville, Kentucky.

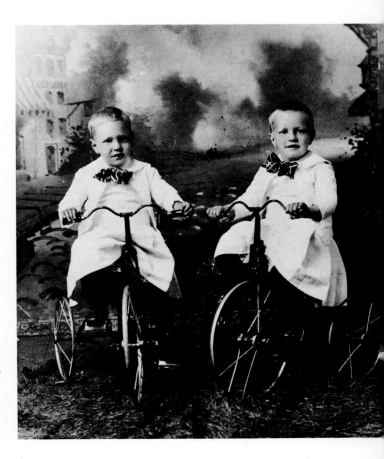

Harrison Thayer of New Cumberland, West Virginia, was caught by Geer & Bricker, Photographers.

A new combination, from a Falmouth, Kentucky, photographic studio, offers a balanced ticket: Harrison Morton Marquardt.

The prize of the collection, from the Odentraggs family of Lyons, Nebraska, is this set of twins, Benjamin and Harrison.

Behind the pomp of the Presidency there lurks the grubbier business of politics, conducted at many levels. Above is one operator par excellence, Senator Chauncey Depew, captured by George Grantham Bain arriving at Saratoga for the New York Republican Convention of 1910. When just out of Yale in 1856, Depew campaigned for the first candidate of the G.O.P., General Frémont; in 1924, at ninety, he was still at it for Coolidge. In 1866, as he was about to accept the job of first United States minister to Japan, Commodore Vanderbilt intercepted him. "Railroads are the career for a young man," said the owner of the New York Central system, then being born. "There is nothing in politics. Don't be a damned fool." Depew became the Central's attorney, and eventually its president, but remained up to his hips in politics.

Somewhat down the political totem pole from Depew's operations was "Big Tim" Sullivan's "shoe line" at Tammany Hall, where faithful ballot-box stuffers are lined up for their reward—and Bain's camera. As candid Tim said, "When you've voted 'em with their whiskers on, you take 'em to a barber and scrape off the chin fringe. Then you vote 'em again with the side lilacs and a mustache. Then to a barber again, off comes the sides and you vote 'em a third time with the mustache. If that ain't enough and the box can stand a few more ballots, clean off the mustache and vote 'em plain face. That makes every one of 'em good for four votes."

Timeless Rituals

No man should enter American politics without durable hands, a strong stomach, and an infinite patience with parades. They are possibly the only absolutely necessary qualifications. The hands outstretched above in a photograph by Bain are determined to seize the hand of William Howard Taft, campaigning in 1908. The gentlemen at left, marching north on Fifth Avenue, a band blaring away behind them, are also for Taft. It is all part of the timeless ritual in every city and every election: the marshal at center in silk hat and sash, his lieutenants only a little less imposing in their derbies. The caption states merely that this is "the Engineer Division." The ancient negative from which this picture was made has deteriorated—making the famous Flatiron Building behind the marchers dim and fuzzy—but the picture is powerful nonetheless.

111

The Also-rans

America is fascinated by its defeated candidates and likes to indulge in long speculations on their misfortunes. In the case of Horatio Seymour, who lost to General Ulysses S. Grant in 1868 by a large electoral majority—although a small popular margin—one question is why the Democratic Party nominated him in the first place, another is why he won as many votes as he did. As Democratic governor of

New York during the Civil War, Seymour was leader of the unpopular opposition to Lincoln. He was opposed to Abolition, thinking slavery would collapse in time of its own weight. He denounced the arrest of Copperheads and other presidential moves he thought beyond constitutional bounds. Nevertheless, he raised troops for the Union armies, and accepted the presidential nomination only with deep misgivings. His diffidence comes through noticeably in these stiff campaign photographs, in which William Kurtz of New York strove to "humanize" the candidate as student of the heavens, hunter, and outdoorsman. "Seymour at Home," Kurtz labeled them, but the "great decliner," which is what irritated fellow Democrats called Seymour, was very clearly not at home in his political role.

If Horatio Seymour was a difficult and diffident subject for the cameraman, so was the man whom the Democrats chose to contest the White House with President Theodore Roosevelt in 1904. The party had wearied of William Jennings Bryan after two defeats; it hoped to attract Republican businessmen smarting under Roosevelt's assaults. And so the convention chose austere Chief Justice Alton B. Parker of the New York Court of Appeals—without really knowing where he stood on public issues. As a judge, Parker had felt he should not make any statements until nominated. But once the choice was made, he dropped a bombshell. He was a sound-money man, devoted to the gold standard—that horrible "cross of gold" so hateful to the Bryanites. The convention swallowed hard and accepted; but the Democratic politicians were again disturbed when the judge for months refused to leave his farm in Esopus, New York, and hit the campaign trail. To be sure, he would speak to visiting groups like the one in the large Underwood & Underwood picture opposite below, but how was the great public ever to see the party's candidate? Off to Esopus went Washington photographer B. M. Clinedinst. The judge posed stiffly (opposite, above), first in a schoolroom chair, reading *Harper's Magazine*. Let us get outdoors, Clinedinst must have thought to himself, but Parker looked no better on an office chair. A rustic chair, a straw hat and a dog were procured, but the unsmiling candidate sat as rigidly as ever. Finally, formidable Mrs. Parker, her daughter, and a clerical son-in-law every inch as frozen-faced as the judge, were marshaled for the photograph at far right, together with two grandchildren. There are no more pictures, for at this moment Clinedinst seems to have accepted defeat. So, in the November election, did Alton B. Parker.

"Theodore! with all thy faults. . . ." This, probably the shortest and most agonized editorial endorsement ever given a candidate, appeared in the conservative New York *Sun* in the Roosevelt-Parker election of 1904. Many people felt the same way about irrepressible "T.R.," the most colorful, the most euphoric, and possibly the most irritating politician ever to occupy the White House. These fine, sharp stereographs enshrine the Rough Rider, below, in an 1898 shot made on his return from Cuba; the big Navy man, left, standing on the bridge of the presidential yacht *Mayflower* and waving his hat at a passing battleship of his Great White Fleet (it is either the *Alabama* or the *Illinois*); and the outdoorsman, hiking at Glacier Point in the Yosemite Valley. Looking at America's new leader after McKinley's assassination, an English paper, borrowing the rhythm from Gilbert and Sullivan, rhymed its comment like this:

> A smack of Lord Cromer, Jeff Davis a touch of him;
> A little of Lincoln, but not very much of him;
> Kitchener, Bismarck and Germany's Will,
> Jupiter, Chamberlain, Buffalo Bill.

Campaign Trails

Crowds, excitement, political uproar, and the glare of publicity followed Theodore Roosevelt from almost his first moments in political life. In the picture at far right he is in full cry, gesturing his way through a speech at Newcastle, Wyoming, during a western tour in 1903. The bunting, the photograph, the reminders of wild life dispatched by the speaker, the local worthies on the platform—all is redolent of politics three-quarters of a century ago, yet it is as alive as the evening newscast on television. Below, drinking in another speech on the same tour (albeit a little conscious of the camera of R. Y. Young, who took both these stereographs), is a Salinas, Kansas, audience of schoolchildren, along with parents and teachers. The West loved T.R., not only for his progressive sympathies but also for the fact that he knew the plains and mountains better than other Presidents; he had ranched and hunted there as a young man. Children loved him for his bounce and his sympathy for them, and indeed he never grew old. As his wife once remarked to a visitor in an irritated moment, "You must remember that the President is only eight years old." Roosevelt was an amateur at everything, as an assemblyman, a historian, a police commissioner, even as a soldier, and he was good at everything, too. For all his many and visible faults, he embodied to his generation the virile America of the early twentieth century.

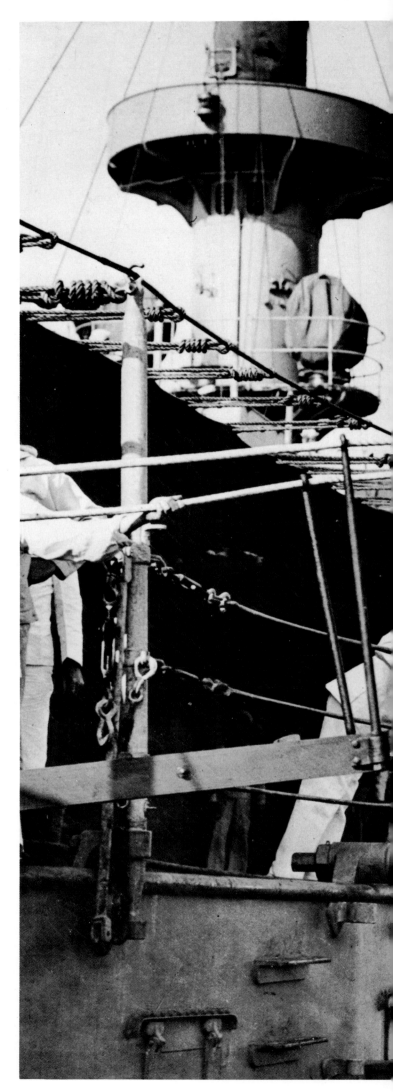

"Big Bill" Taft was third in a line of judges, and loved nothing better than the bench. He had the friendly good nature that makes fat men popular, but he also had great abilities as a peacemaker and a coordinator. That was nearly his undoing: President McKinley sent him in 1900 to govern the Philippines, and he did so well that President Theodore Roosevelt made him secretary of war in 1904. In that capacity he revisited our "little brown brothers" (as he called them) in 1905—the misspelled and somewhat unstuck welcoming arch above greeted him at Iloilo during that trip. The picture is by Burr McIntosh. Taft also kept tabs on the progress of Panama Canal construction; on the opposite page he is crossing a gangplank between ships on that assignment. Since Roosevelt had incautiously announced he would not seek a third term, he pushed Taft forward to an easy victory over William Jennings Bryan in 1908. Big Bill struggled with the presidency while T.R. went big-game hunting in Africa (J. P. Morgan hoped to a friend that "some lion will do its duty"). A marked coolness soon grew up between Taft and Roosevelt, culminating in a party split in 1912, Roosevelt's run on the Progressive ticket, and a minority victory by the patrician Democrat Woodrow Wilson. Poor Taft ran third, but ended his life happily when appointed, in 1921, as Chief Justice of the United States, the biggest job he ever really wanted.

Imperial America

After Appomattox faded into history and in the long years before the American Expeditionary Force left for France, war seemed to most Americans a rather far-off, perhaps hazardous, but certainly romantic business. It made heroes like Roosevelt and Admiral Dewey and George Armstrong Custer, gave us tunes to whistle, and colored in as American a few places on the map that had not already been taken over by Britain and other imperial powers. A great deal of the photography—like the reports of a new breed of war correspondents—was romantic. The scene in the Philippines at the left, copyrighted in 1899 by Perley Fremont Rockett, belongs in that genre, and is captioned "Taking it easy during a lull." Below is a rather more grisly scene, skulls of what the caption calls simply "Spanish-American War Victims, Cristobal Colon Cemetery, Havana." Cubans killed by Spaniards? Spaniards killed by Americans? Americans? The last is unlikely; there would have been a scandal, since we do not, like Latin countries, keep ossuaries. The question hangs in the air, as it does with many old photographs in the Library of Congress received in the days before modern research and cataloguing. But the picture speaks its message clearly enough: the romance had its price.

The result of the Spanish-American War back home was a brisk battle between "imperialists" and "anti-imperialists" over whether to keep the loot. In the end we kept it. Some people read Kipling's poem "Recessional" and spent many years thereafter worrying about what else we had acquired along with dominion over palm and pine. Another minor result was a proliferation of bad poetry and worse symbolic photography of the variety displayed here. Our two selections from this genre include a stereograph called "Waiting for Uncle Sam— On the Beach, Porto Rico" by B. L. Singley, put out in 1900 by the Keystone View Company, and a large composite photoprint made in 1898 by George Prince of Washington, D.C., under the grandiose title "Dawn of Day in the Antilles." His Columbia, one must admit, is a smashing young woman.

VI. *Rank and Station*

The gentleman facing us at left, we feel fairly safe in asserting, is the very prototype of an American aristocrat at the time, in 1902, when he sat for this portrait by Purdy of Boston. The patrician nose, the fur-lined greatcoat, the horseshoe stickpin, the general air of hauteur, all reinforce our assertion—although we know only the sitter's name, C. A. P. Talbot. At the risk of inaccuracy as to the man himself, however, it is possible to point to him as a type not contemplated by the egalitarians of the American Revolution—not, certainly, part of Jefferson's society of small farmers, mechanics, and artisans. The real aristocrats of those times, supposedly, had sailed away with His Majesty's ships, back to the highly stratified world of England. None of that Old World nonsense here. From the very beginning, in actuality, the New World had its class structure, beginning with the Pilgrims, divided between the "saints" (or members of the church) and the professional soldiers, artisans, and lowly nonmembers who accompanied them. Jefferson himself was a squire and a slaveholder; John Hancock, whose bold signature leads all the rest on the Declaration of Independence, was the richest man in Boston. Rank and station are, of course, products of money, position, and land, if held on to and properly distilled by time. Until the rise of great wealth in the nineteenth century, to be sure, squire and yeoman knew each other; merchant and artisan, employer and employee, even (in the South) black and white lived not far apart on farms and in villages and towns. If that intimacy passed with the rise of great cities, it remained true that the time required to make it from the bottom of the ladder to the top was, in this land of fast-rising fortunes, the shortest in history. One generation sufficed, or at most two—although, of course, precedence (how long have you had the money?) meant that Mrs. Astor looked down on the newer Vanderbilts and in turn was scorned by the poorer but prouder Knickerbocker aristocracy. Society, whether the word be capitalized or not, has always been a rabbit warren of degrees, layers, and shadings and not simply a matter of three set classes, upper, middle, and lower— a situation from which no nation in the world is exempt, or even wants to be. The pictures in this chapter are concerned with extremes, from the visibly poor to the obviously rich. It is interesting to speculate into which rank or station the descendants of these people, indeed those of many others in this book, may have risen or declined in ensuing generations. For example, what became of the Talbot family, or the little boys named for President Harrison, or the Hearsts?

Elegant C. A. P. Talbot, opposite, looks out loftily from one of many fine portraits of Boston notables taken by the firm of J. E. Purdy.

The grand room at left, which escapes any exact stylistic description except, perhaps, baronial, is the library in the Washington home of Phoebe Apperson Hearst, the widow of Senator George Hearst. If it seems a little short on books, it is long on heavy, ornate furniture and thickly displayed art. Nothing to match the Astors or Vanderbilts of New York in display (Phoebe's son, William Randolph Hearst, would catch up in time), but quite sufficient to prove that a family could make it in America in one generation. Her husband went to California in 1850 and struck it rich in the mines—developing among others the Ophir, the Homestake, and the Anaconda— then went on to the United States Senate. His serious, much younger wife became an important philanthropist in her own right. This photograph is one of many similar interior views done on commissions by Frances Benjamin Johnston.

Perhaps the most ancient hallmark of aristocracy is ownership and graceful use of the horse. Medieval knights rode, while hinds and yeomen walked. In crowded New York at the turn of the century, an unhandy place for ordinary horseback riding, the best way to display one's equine connections was at the relatively new sport of coaching. Its wealthy enthusiasts, with horses, harness, and equipage gleaming, would set out to make a day of it, following the old, half-forgotten stagecoach routes to country points, a picturesque undertaking that vanished with the advent of modern traffic. This happy group in 1906, from the Bain collection, includes Miss Angelica Gerry at the reins, her brother Robert and sister Mabel, and two unidentified guests. The first notable Gerry was a revolutionist from the beginnings of the troubles with the British Crown, a signer of the Declaration of Independence, and Madison's Vice-President; his son was a philanthropist, a founder of the Society for the Prevention of Cruelty to Children, launched in 1874 and called the "Gerry Society."

Running down the long ladder of social levels in America from the ostentatious wealth of Fifth and Park avenues, the opposite extreme could be found not far away in the same city. At right, for example, is the tenement home of a family named Chinquanana, at 11 Hamilton Street in New York, in a photograph taken by one of the first documentary photographers driven by a social conscience, Lewis Wickes Hine. Born in Oshkosh, Wisconsin, in 1874, Hine came to New York in 1901 to teach at the Ethical Culture School and slipped almost accidentally into photography, focusing his camera on the immigrants pouring into Ellis Island, and then the working classes all over America. Animated by the same cause as the more famous Jacob Riis, Hine was the better photographer.

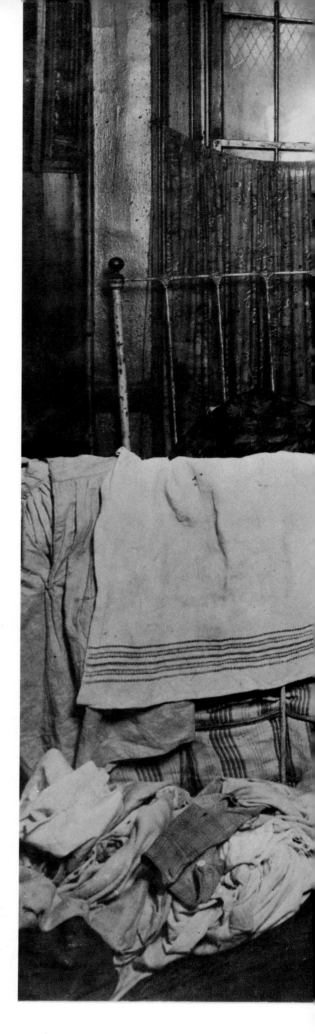

PRODUCTS OF THE TENEMENT WORKSHOP

Flannel Sacque
Worker paid 12¢ a dozen
Retail Selling Price 1⁰⁰ Each
12 hours the working day
62½¢ the day's earnings.
Work: Sew garment together, trim.
Add hooks and eyes.
Worker supplies thread.

Glove Finishing
Work: hand-sewing tapes under buttons
Amount paid varies 6¢-13¢ a doz. pairs
Average daily earnings for 3 persons work 60¢
Family of 5 sleep in room
where work is done.
License Refused.

Chiffon Applique
Work: Sprays and leaves cut from
Chiffon and joined.
Worker Paid 6¢ a yard.
Average out put per hour ⅚ yard.
Worker buys scissors, 50¢ and
pays for sharpening 20¢ a month.

Infants Dress (D)
10¢ a dozen (⅚ a piece)
3½¢ an hour, rate of earnings.
14 to 16 hours the working day
50 pieces the day's work, during rush season
50¢ the day's earnings.
Retail price 1⁰⁰

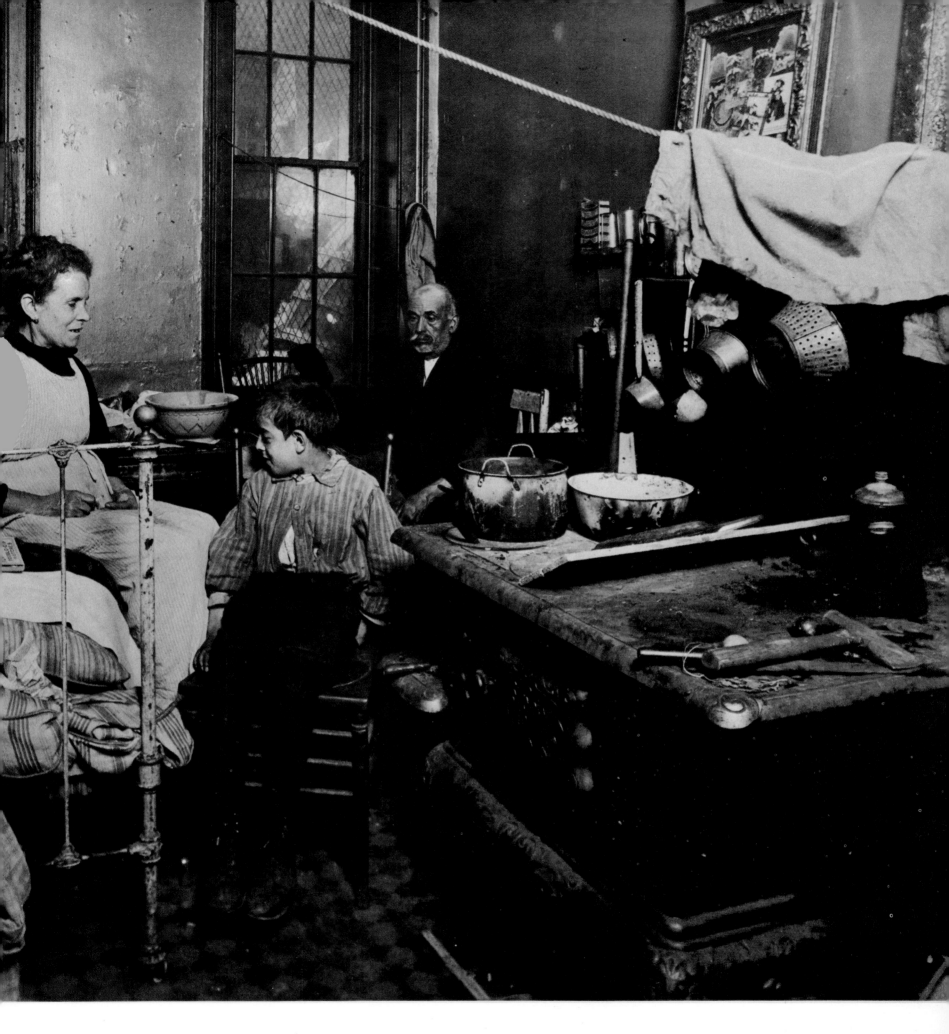

Hine turned over to reformist movements his tenement photographs and the pathetic exhibits he collected. In the case of the photograph at left, it was to the Consumers' League in New York, a group fighting against tenement workshops. Giving up teaching in 1908, Hine took a job with the National Child Labor Committee and for the next ten years traveled the country, documenting the evils of the system that wore out children before they reached adulthood. Mines, factories, can-neries—where children as young as ten labored six days a week and as long as fourteen hours a day—became his stalking grounds. It was often necessary for him to disguise himself from the owners as a salesman of Bibles, a fire inspector, or an industrial photographer. Enough more of his work appears later in this book to prove that Hine was a fine artist with the camera as well as a crusader. But there was no money in the work, and he died in poverty in 1940, his name little known.

131

Men of Property

What counted with men of property at the turn of the century was propriety; the vulgarities of the Gilded Age were behind them. Rockefeller had propriety, Carnegie had it, and J. Pierpont Morgan the Elder, left, had the most of all. The picture, from an old stereograph, was probably never circulated because it displays all too uncharitably the famous Morgan nose, whose skin affliction doubtless accounted for some of Mr. Morgan's dislike of photographers. It was 1908, and Morgan, at Yale to receive an honorary degree, is shaking hands with Yale's president-to-be, William Howard Taft. The man between them, despite the resemblance, is not Mark Twain but Samuel J. Elder, a then famous trial lawyer and raconteur.

Unlike J. P. Morgan, Andrew Carnegie delighted in the public eye. Below, he is standing at right on the platform with folded arms and a pleased expression, enjoying the procession at the twenty-fifth anniversary of the founding of Tuskegee Institute in 1906. Having relished the collection of wealth, he was now with equal zest setting about spending almost all of it on good causes. At the far left is Robert C. Ogden, a long-time benefactor of education for southern blacks, but there is no sign of Tuskegee's founder, Booker T. Washington, in this strangely segregated scene—all apparently white on the reviewing stand, all black in the procession. This is one of many Tuskegee pictures by the gifted Frances Benjamin Johnston.

Banqueters

Our grandfathers' and great-grandfathers' generations liked to break bread together, and to do it frequently in large groups and odd circumstances. This impulse is attested by considerable files of large, tattered group photographs that can be unearthed here and there in the files of the Library of Congress. There are banquets for personages, mostly forgotten, for reunions, for commerce, for like-minded groups of all kinds—large, sepia, crumbly scenes of mass mastication which someone once thought should be recorded for posterity. The banqueters wear strange costumes, funny hats or grapes in their hair, or affect other fancies, although they rarely stray out of white or black ties. The scene at left, labeled merely "The Banquet," was copyrighted in 1903 by R. Newell & Son of Philadelphia. Too big to be jockeys, the diners are clearly horsemen, and their horses are included in the festivities. In the 1910 Lewis Hine photograph below, two brothers on a New York Street are banqueting less formally than either the men or their horses on discarded fruit outside a Fourteenth Street market. The boy behind is, Hine records, most regrettably stealing some good fruit out of a basket.

Portraits

Every period of history, whether it scowls or smiles, has its own idea of what makes a fetching portrait, although historians of photography would assert that the poses have originated with the people behind the camera rather than those in front. This selection, taken about eighty years ago, is part of the vast and still not fully sorted files of the talented photographer Frances Benjamin Johnston, whose wide-ranging work appears throughout this book. Each of the ladies emerges with a distinctive charm, for all the differences in style; the pictures are probably proofs, and the young girl at bottom left appears in a cyanotype, or blueprint. They are captioned, simply, "Miss Barney" (top left), "Miss Brewster" (bottom left), "Misses Blount" (below), one reading, one thinking, and "Miss Apperson" (at right). The quotes are the photographer's, and the caption indicates that the banjo player is performing beside a statue of Flora in the Hearst residence in Washington, whose library is shown earlier in this chapter. Since the real Miss Apperson married Hearst in 1862, this young lady of 1900 may be a young relative taking part in some sort of charade or home theatrical performance.

At some remove from the elegant young ladies of Washington on the preceding pages, indeed far across the tracks from them, are these spinners of 1910 at a cotton mill in Knoxville, Tennessee. Despite the romantic view of "southern

womanhood" so long prevalent in America, a more somber actuality is revealed in the child labor pictures of Lewis Hine.

Of course, such girls would be worn out before their time, yet humanity asserts itself, and the pretty waifs here are smiling.

Poor Little Rich Boy

It is very difficult to smile, in fact you just won't smile, when the photographer follows you around all day and tries to make you. Besides, you have to be all dressed up, and not get dirty, just when you wanted to do something else. . . . It *is* difficult to be rich, and little, and have your play organized. These photographs, captioned "Master McLean," are from the McLean Collection in the Library of Congress, and give interesting glimpses, albeit usually uncaptioned, of the family of Edward Beale ("Ned") McLean, a poor little rich boy himself who inherited the Washington *Post* and Cincinnati *Enquirer* from his father. McLean married Evalyn, daughter of the millionaire mining king, Tom Walsh. One result of the union was "Master McLean," Vinson Walsh McLean, shown at left with his mother being pushed about in Palm Beach, Florida; at right he poses with his little play cottage, top, and his lion cubs. Alas, such happy times were not to last. Not long after the young master's birth in 1909, Evalyn had bought herself the famous Hope Diamond, supposed bringer of bad luck. The diamond kept its reputation: in 1919, while his parents were away at the Kentucky Derby, the boy darted across a Georgetown street and was killed by a passing Model T. Several years later, foolish Ned got tangled up in the Teapot Dome scandal by trying to help out his thieving friend, Secretary of the Interior Albert Fall.

Below a certain age a good city puddle will do for a pond, a stray dog is as serviceable as pet lion cubs—better, perhaps—and it is nice not to have supervision all the time. Unfortunately, however, as the statistics on poverty and juvenile delinquency make clear, the advantages of low station don't last. This unidentified New York scene is by George Grantham Bain.

Outside the factory gates in South Bend, Indiana, in 1914 a little girl pauses beneath the warm and welcoming sign of the Singer Sewing Machine Company. Whether she is bringing in her father's lunch or on her way to work herself no one can say. When the photographer, Lewis Hine, could not gain access to his child labor studies any other way, he took his camera to factory gateways or to workers' homes. Besides its obvious message, this photograph displays Hine's great artistry.

OVERLEAF: At a cigarette factory in Danville, Virginia, Hine took this picture of girls during their lunch period—or what his sardonic caption calls their "noon recreation." In many ways Hine anticipated the natural style of modern photography.

VII. E Pluribus Not Quite Unum

You are the buffalo-ghost, the broncho-ghost
With dollar-silver in your saddle-horn,
The cowboys riding in from Painted Post,
The Indian arrow in the Indian corn. . . .

Stepchild of every exile from content
And all the disavouched, hard-bitten pack
Shipped overseas to steal a continent
With neither shirts nor honor to their back. . . .

Puritans stubborn as the nails of Pride,
Rakes from Versailles and thieves from County
* Clare. . . .*

The black-robed priests who broke their hearts in
* vain*
To make you God and France or God and Spain.
                                    —Stephen Vincent Benét

Our national motto, of course, refers to the various states that joined to make up the federal union, but it applies equally well to all the different peoples that, we like to feel, have joined to form one united nation. After an initial period of petulance and skepticism about each other's prerogatives, the states got along well enough; the people are a different story. From the beginning there was friction. The native Americans' resentment of the European newcomers erupted immediately—and remains alive even after four centuries of war and extermination. In turn, the early English settlers mocked the Germans when they arrived; the Germans hated the Irish; the Irish hated the Italians; and nearly everyone hated the Jews. "The scum of creation has been dumped upon us," said a turn-of-the-century politician, welcoming the southern Europeans then pouring into the simmering confusion of New York's Lower East Side. "The most dangerous and corrupting hordes of the Old World have invaded us." Yet, for all the venom, there remained something oddly heartening about the process; however badly it worked, it was something of a miracle that it worked at all. The luckless gentleman who made the crossing in 1755 to escape his gambling debts and the Sicilian farmer whose land finally gave out in 1890 came spurred by a common goad: a fresh chance, a shot at something better. Some immigrants and racial groups rose rapidly, others made little or no progress, but all were shaped and changed by the experience. Hundreds of photographers recorded their travails, and the Library of Congress has thousands of pictures that are particularly revelatory, not only because they show the immigrant's lot as it was, but because they also show it as others wanted to see it. So, along with studies of slum conditions, there are fantasies calculated to soothe and amuse. For the southerner, there were vignettes of loyal, happy, foolish, harmless Negroes, and, for northern consumption, those same blacks reading up on Abe Lincoln, well on the way to success and equality. By the turn of the century the Indian, that remorseless heathen hated by virtually all the settlers who took his lands, had become a reminder of a colorful past, to be posed and photographed in all his savagery. Along with such carefully composed curiosities are true glimpses of the Indian, broken and sunk in apathy, of the Italian struggling in his tenement workshop, and of all the other disparate people on whose dreams and frustrations our troubled, vital republic was built.

The great Hunkpapa Sioux chief Sitting Bull had been hounded into surrender by 1882 when the Dakota Territory firm of Bailey, Dix & Mead took this picture of him and his family sitting by their tepee at Fort Randall. The white woman is a Boston widow named Catherine Weldon, a somewhat neurotic do-gooder who lavished attention on the deposed chief until he proposed making her his third wife.

The Face of the Sioux

Scarcely a generation before an Omaha photographer named Frank Rinehart took these portraits of Sioux Indians in 1899, the mighty tribe had dominated the northern plains from the upper Missouri down to the Platte River. The Sioux had fought the white man longer than any other Plains tribe, until the struggle ended before a battery of Hotchkiss guns at Wounded Knee. Though little of defeat can be read on the faces of Lost Horse, opposite, and Tall Red Bird, above, the nineteen thousand survivors from their nation had been scattered onto South Dakota reservations. "They made us many promises," said one old Sioux, "more than I can remember, but they never kept but one; they promised to take our land and they took it." These two men, born to be warriors, were shipped in as living artifacts to the Omaha International Exposition. And for all their pride and noble bearing, they stood docile while the photographer arranged their costumes so as to appeal to his sense of the picturesque.

Here are two more of Rinehart's Indian studies, which are part of a series of some four hundred, virtually all of them of Sioux, copyrighted during 1899 and 1900 by Heyn and Heyn & Matzen of Omaha. At left, a young warrior peers out from beneath a superb headdress, at the ready for a battle he will never fight. Plump, healthy-looking little John Lone Bull, at right, faces a grim future; the late 1890's were a bleak time to be born into a western tribe. Under the heedless supervision of the United States government, on one reservation a similar youngster managed to survive the bitter winters by huddling on straw between mongrel dogs, his family too poor to buy beds, stoves, or even blankets.

Concerned Parents

The members of this dignified group are Black-foot chiefs on a trip east in 1892 to see how their children are faring learning white men's ways at the Carlisle Indian Industrial School. The famous Pennsylvania institution, the first nonreservation Indian school, had been founded on cavalry lieutenant Richard Henry Pratt's conviction that native prisoners in his care could be better handled through kindness and instruction than through intimidation. He badgered the government into supplying funds, took over an old Army post, and opened his school late in 1879. Described in his day as "the red man's Moses," the well-intentioned Pratt chose students from the western tribes, brought them to Pennsylvania, cropped their hair, gave them white man's names, and pressed them to abandon the follies of their own culture. Some—the great athlete Jim Thorpe among them—did well enough for a while. Others sank into resentful torpor. Their reluctance is perhaps mirrored in this group of visitors—only two of the eight deigned to put on white man's clothes when they sat for the school's official photographer, J. N. Choate. The chiefs are, from left to right, Running Crane, White Grass, Four Horses, Little Dog (sitting), Brochy, White Calf, Bear Chief, and Little Plume. The school closed in 1918. Today the Carlisle Barracks houses the United States Army War College. There is a small graveyard behind the college whose tombstones bear such names as Nora Izancho and Laura Lumpfoot—victims of white man's diseases.

Black Stereotypes

In 1889 Henry Grady, the Atlanta newspaper editor, concluded happily that "the Negro as a political force has dropped out of serious consideration." The threat of a black franchise had largely passed in the South, and northern pressure to improve the lot of the Negro, fairly strong following the Civil War, had waned. A great many white Southerners were deeply relieved that the status quo and the Ku Klux Klan had prevailed. They did not hate Negroes; there were good ones and bad ones. The bad ones got the chain gang and the rope, the good ones the sort of sentimental eulogizing shown in these two photographs. The small boy above, reverently studying the picture of Lincoln, was photographed in 1901 by J. H. Tarbell, a North Carolina cameraman who had a northern audience in mind for that particular picture. The sweet old family retainer comes from the studio of O. Pierre Havens of Jacksonville, Florida. Whatever other purposes these stereotypes served, they also helped stave off the fear of black assertion that permeated the South—and the North. In 1892, when Havens took the picture at left, patronizingly entitled "The Good Old Kind," a record one hundred sixty-one blacks were lynched.

At the turn of the century, photographers were turning out "colored comics" by the thousands, which comforted and amused their audience by showing blacks to be an affable, lazy people, bemused by common phenomena, inordinately fond of chicken and watermelon, scared of ghosts, given to ludicrous illiterate circumlocutions, and generally feckless. The blacks themselves, adept at surviving the brutal caprices of their world, often appeared to go along with the shuffling charade; at best, it brought them a measure of peace. The old preacher, taken by McGrory and Company of Atlanta, is, according to the caption that accompanied the original picture, saying, "I don't see de word about [stealing] chicken nowhere." The girl at right, taken from a Keystone stereograph, is asking "Don't Dolly Look Like Me?", while the bizarre fantasy below, another Havens opus, is labeled "The Florida Toboggan."

Black Realities

Thirty years after the arrival of Northern armies and emancipation, most southern blacks had gained little more than a transition from slavery to serfdom. For every one who earned a wage, many more grubbed from small parcels of ground landowners rented to them in return for a share of the crop. The crop usually was cotton, and so many farmers produced it that prices often sank far below the cost of production. White sharecroppers had a bad time of it, too, but blacks tended to get the worst of the disastrous economics of tenant farming. Meanwhile, the Supreme Court dedicated the last quarter of the nineteenth century to emasculating the civil rights acts passed by the Reconstruction Congresses of the 1870's. Thus the life of the southern black remained the struggle shown in these pictures by J. H. Tarbell, the North Carolinian who produced the study of the worshipful black boy kneeling before Lincoln. Hoping, perhaps, to sell these pictures to the same audience, Tarbell gave his portrait of these grave children the title "Three Little Coons."

When the United States prodded Spain into war in 1898, black men joined the Army—whereupon the photographers' chicken-stealing simpleton became one of "our brave colored boys." But not right away, and not to everyone; while in training the men of the 24th Infantry, shown here in a Keystone stereograph view by B. L. Singley, erupted in a race riot after white Ohio troops who had "decided to have some fun" fired at a two-year-old black boy. Despite such incidents, the 24th fought hard and well in Cuba. "I must say that I never saw braver men anywhere," said Rough Rider Frank Knox. But when the troops got home, they found things much the same. One southerner complained to a reporter that all the "fuss" about black troops "has set up the . . . Negroes . . . in their own estimation, and its effect upon them has been bad." But despite this sort of sentiment, there were spots in the country—some midwestern small towns, for instance—where blacks were just citizens like everybody else, getting along as best they could. That rare and happy situation is reflected in the quiet scene below, which the Wright Brothers included in their album. It shows Alonzo and Clarence Tucker, no better or worse dressed than any of the other kids in Dayton, sitting on a bench behind the celebrated bicycle shop.

Mysterious Albums

What might be called the Tuskegee ethic is mirrored in these two pictures, exhibiting them as aspiring members of the middle class, with its manners and graces—even though the setting for the piano lesson at the left seems (on close inspection) to be a standard photographer's backdrop of the period. The photographs are part of a large group, untitled and uncaptioned, found bound into a set of large, elegant blue volumes, each stamped in gold with the name of the late W. E. B. Du Bois. The photographs show many aspects of life among blacks in the early 1900's in Georgia—rich and poor, slums and nice houses. One volume contains copies of old-time "black codes" and other laws affecting race, but there is no explanation of the photographs, no writing to indicate how the collection, now falling apart, came to the Library of Congress. It is possible that the work was part of certain researches into the life of the black race that Du Bois carried on in the period while he was at Atlanta University. Du Bois was an angrier, more radical leader than patient Booker T. Washington. What was the purpose of the albums? Who gave them to the library? There are no answers.

165

Striving Forward

Nineteenth-century orthodoxy held that if blacks were really to rise, they had to do so within the framework of white society. "In all things purely social," said Booker T. Washington in 1895, "we can be as separate as the fingers, yet one as the hand in all things essential to mutual progress." In other words, give us jobs, and we won't bother you. That this attitude is today outmoded in no way dims the achievement of Washington, who, born a slave, managed to educate himself and eventually to become superintendent of Tuskegee Institute. In 1881, working without funds, he enrolled the first seventeen students in the abandoned Alabama plantation house that served as his inaugural school building. By the turn of the century, Tuskegee was educating twelve hundred blacks. Something of this energy—and of the allegiance to white custom on which it was founded—can be read in these two portraits by Frances Benjamin Johnston. Below is John H. Washington, Tuskegee's Superintendent of Industries and, at right, the scientist George Washington Carver, who first came to Tuskegee to teach and experiment in 1896 and who had become a national legend when he died on the campus in 1943.

Separate and Unequal

Despite the best efforts of Tuskegee, the brief wartime gains, and the occasional benignity of the small towns, the blacks were only slightly more successful than the Indians in overcoming their old miseries—as these pictures, the most recent in the book, suggest. They were taken by photographers working for the Farm Security Administration's monumental survey of American life during the 1930's and early 1940's. Jack Delano photographed the hands reaching through the bars in Green County, Georgia, in 1941, and the same year recorded the Oglethorpe County, Georgia, work gang. Marion Post Wolcott took the picture of the segregated movie theater in Belzoni, Mississippi, in 1939.

At the Golden Door

The last part of the nineteenth century saw a great influx of "new immigrants"—people from southern and eastern Europe—much to the dismay of the established northern European stock, whose own ancestors had fled land taxes and the debtor's prison a few generations earlier. The newcomers passed into the country through more than seventy processing centers, but three-quarters of them came in via the most famous station of them all—Ellis Island in New York Harbor. That is where the Italian family at left was photographed. They have been cleared for landing in Manhattan, and face the baffling rigors of their new land armed only with the possessions they have been able to fit into their bundles. They will probably find themselves part of the swarming life of New York's Lower East Side, whose tenements absorbed hordes of recent arrivals; with a thousand people per square acre, it was the most densely populated spot in the world. Of the solemn children below we know nothing at all, except that they were photographed around 1915 by George Grantham Bain.

Here Come the Brides

The radiant young immigrant woman above has a specific goal in mind for her American adventure, and almost certainly she will achieve it. She is one of 1,002 women who arrived aboard the White Star liner *Baltic* seeking American husbands. When the ship docked September 27, 1907, a band was waiting, and a good number of hopeful bachelors were milling about on the pier. Word had spread far; the State Board of Immigration of Michigan, anxious to increase the population around Kalamazoo, had sent a delegation of young farmers charged with the responsibility of convincing the women that northern Michigan was the Eden of the New World. But many of the girls weren't buying. This was definitely true of Clara McGee from Roscommon; though she had never set foot in a theater, she announced her determination to become a famous actress. Others, having assessed what was important in the United States, said they would settle only for railroad engineers or skyscraper builders. One pragmatic Liverpudlian said flatly, "It's a Pittsburgh millionaire for me," and Gena Jensen from Oslo refused all blandishments "because there is someone waiting for me in a place called Connecticut." The group on the opposite page had a surer thing than the *Baltic* brides; when they came from England in 1911 their way had been paved in advance, and their fiancés were waiting for them. A photographer for the firm of Underwood & Underwood took this picture before the women moved off the pier and into wedlock.

174

The Chinese did not begin to emigrate to America until the mid-nineteenth century, when reports of gold in California lured them across the Pacific. Even then they did not come to settle. Tied to their native land by strong bonds of tradition and religion, they intended to make their fortunes and return to China. Encouraged by boosterish circulars ("Americans are very rich people. They want the Chinaman to come and will make him welcome. . . . It will not be a strange country"), they found themselves savagely resented by native Americans. Given only the toughest, dirtiest jobs of digging and earth-hauling, the Chinese doggedly got the work done. Though they clung to their native clothing and customs, somewhere along the line many of them ceased to be visitors and became settlers, a transformation that is suggested by the stalwart hose team at left, photographed in 1888 by J. C. H. Grabill. According to his caption, these men are "The champion Chinese hose team of America, who won the great Hub-and-Hub race at Deadwood, Dakota Terr. July 4." Eventually economic depression and mounting prejudice squeezed the Chinese out of towns like Deadwood and into the cities. The people below were photographed in San Francisco's crowded Chinatown in 1901 by a cameraman named C. H. Graves.

Beyond the port cities the immediate destination was, for many immigrant children, some factory town. This predominantly Italian group of boys was photographed by Hine in 1911 at the Ayer Mill in Lawrence, Massachusetts. He recorded their names, but only eleven of them for twelve boys, so that one can only guess who is who: Joe Christy, Harold Old, Sam Gangi, Wallace Hogan, Sebastino Genovese, Leopoldo Andreoli, Uroli Farealla, Salvatore Finechelli, Joseph D'Angelo, Pasuala Dearndo. Being boys, one or two of them mugged and played tough. What happened to these poignant offshoots of sunny Italy in cold and grimy Lawrence one would like to know but cannot find out. Nevertheless, in a generation or two the Italians bootstrapped themselves forward in economic and political influence, as had the Irish before them.

Green Power

The Irish were held together in the New World—to a degree that worried the older, Protestant stock—by the well-organized Roman Catholic church, shown in full panoply here on the steps of St. Patrick's Cathedral in New York on a June day in 1916. The picture was taken while the 69th Infantry, called "The Fighting Irish" in those old ethnic, nonintegrated days, was marching past. And as pictures go, it is eloquent. At the center, with a top hat and a flag, is Monsignor Michael Joseph Lavelle, a contractor's son who frequently had to explain that he was not French and that "Lavelle" is derived from the Gaelic. When the cornerstone of St. Patrick's, symbol of Catholic power in New York, was laid in 1858, Lavelle attended on his father's shoulders. Now he was its parish priest, or rector. The archives of the Archdiocese of New York identify also, on Lavelle's left, Monsignor Joseph P. Dineen, holding his boater, and the Reverend Bernard McQuade; and on his right, the Reverend John J. Byrne and the Reverend Francis P. Duffy. Duffy, grandson of an immigrant during the famous famine, was one of eleven children born in poverty and, being frail, was given to the church. (It was his good fortune, for five of the little Duffys died in childhood.) When the 69th went to the Mexican border and then overseas, Father Duffy went along as chaplain and won lasting fame for his cheery, hard-boiled manner, his courage, and his ability to get on with anyone. In time, there were medals, a statue, a Hollywood movie about him, and, finally, a military funeral that was held in this same cathedral, with twenty-five thousand in attendance.

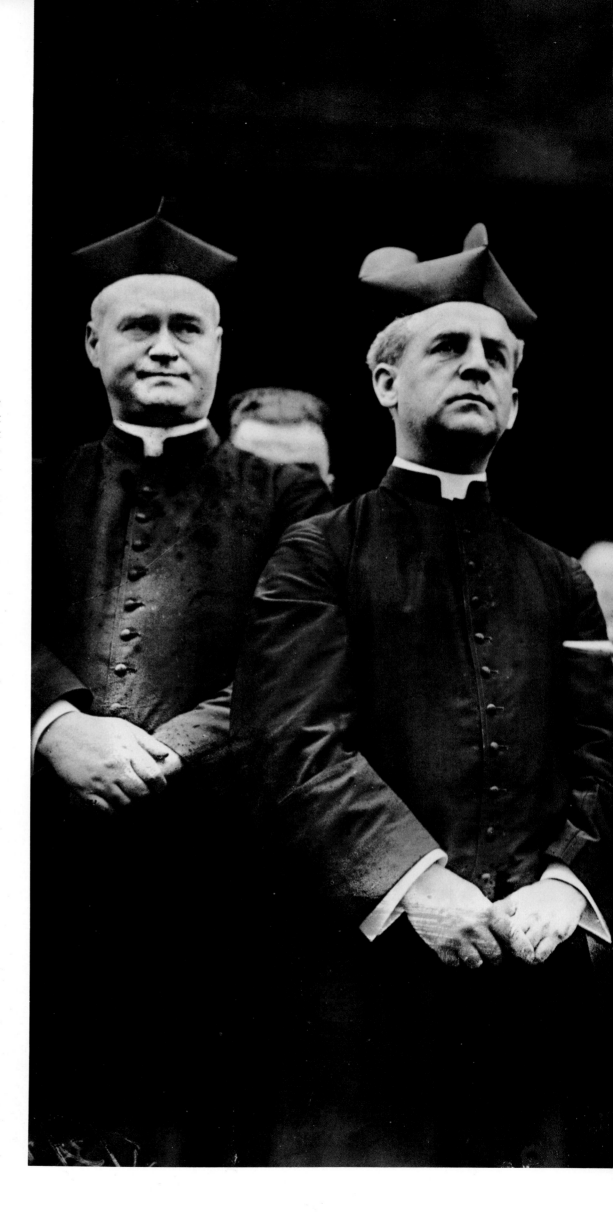

179

VIII. Male and Female Created He Them

A man is in general better pleased when he has a good dinner upon his table, than when his wife talks Greek.
—Samuel Johnson

As almost any prophet could have told you at the close of the nineteenth century—a time of much self-conscious looking forward—almost everything in the world was changing. But if you could have shown him the picture at left he might have added, "Except that." Love, marriage, the relationship of the sexes: these were ordained like the stars above. Woman's place was fixed, beside her man, whether that meant slaving in poverty or idling away her days on a pedestal in a rich man's home. Man was the provider, and woman managed the home, saw to the meals, and brought up the children. The noted writer on the home, Catharine Beecher, put it this way: "The family state is the aptest earthly illustration of the heavenly kingdom, and in it woman is its chief minister." Since Miss Beecher, a lifelong spinster herself, had grown up in a family of preachers (among them Henry Ward Beecher), suffragists (like sister Isabel), and reformers (like sister Harriet Beecher Stowe, who earned the living in *her* family), this might have been thought to be the last word on the subject. But the job of "chief minister" was difficult and sometimes unbearable. Hard-working wives wore out early, idle ones lived unhealthy, inactive lives. Repressed in the matter of sex, which lay under a taboo and could scarcely be mentioned in polite society, restrained from anything but genteel—or humble—activities, only lightly educated in comparison with men of equal station, disenfranchised, imprisoned in her corsets, American woman was a kind of time bomb waiting to explode. Although it was rarely their purpose, photographers of the Victorian Age have accidentally left us a bulging file on the sexes in their time. These pictures offer a lively contrast to the twentieth century, when women have become well over a third of the national work force and when almost no door remains closed to them. To the 1970's, accustomed to "women's lib," not to mention a great deal of noise and exhibitionism as women burst into bars and clubs, all exaggerated by the excited attentions of television, the pictures in this chapter may seem unduly quaint. Perhaps they are; it is hard sometimes to resist preposterous scenes because they so underscore a point. Sometimes, too, they make another point, hard to perceive amidst the heat and inflated language of the sexual revolution, which is that there is often more ado on the tube, and in the newspapers, than there is in the lives of ordinary people.

This wonderful romantic moment—he all sheep's eyes, she demure, their friend amused—was photographed in 1890 by a skilled amateur named Emma Justine Farnsworth, who was active between 1886 and 1902. Over two hundred of her glass plates, tintypes, and film negatives were presented to the library by a kinsman in 1952. They include many fine groups and posed genre studies like this one.

Front, back, sideways, from every angle, photographers have always celebrated the female of the species; in that, at least, she has perhaps been more equal than the male. The determined feminist will assert that this is to treat women as sex objects, or some kind of toy, an argument which we had best pursue no further. Under whichever theory one operates, it is clear that two girls only multiply the charm or exploitation. The sweet-faced sisters above, by an unknown photographer, are the Misses Grace, left, and Emma Marie Bird of Asbury Park, New Jersey—a casual portrait taken perhaps when they were out for a stroll. Every device of artistry and preparation, however, has gone into the lovely study opposite of the Gerson sisters, belles of the art world at the turn of the century, in costumes for the Crinoline Ball. The photographer herself, Gertrude Stanton Käsebier, was something of a revolutionary. As a child she had gone west to Leadville, Colorado, in a covered wagon. Later, when her widowed mother was operating a boarding house in New York, she met Eduard Käsebier, a shellac importer, raised a family, and then somewhat defiantly took up first painting and then, in 1897, photography. Plump and forty-five, she opened a studio on Fifth Avenue. It prospered. In 1902 Mrs. Käsebier joined with Alfred Stieglitz, Edward Steichen, and other famous photographers in the Photo-Secession group, with new ideas of what constituted art in photography. Her clean, imaginative work won her an international reputation, one of the first for an American woman in the creative professions.

DO NOT THROW
STONES OVER
THE CLIFF.

Two by Two

Not just their clothes, but an almost terrifying innocence separates the newly married of long ago from their late-twentieth-century counterparts. In the simple wedding picture of an unknown couple at right—from an old *carte de visite*—the bride's hand lies both timidly and tentatively on her husband's shoulder; both of them stare into space. And who can fail to be affected by the two honeymoon couples on the facing page, doing their obligatory tourist rounds at Niagara Falls—two by two, like so many passengers in Noah's Ark, happy but uncertain. The two viewing points are on Goat Island, looking northward past the American Falls. In the background is the Upper Steel Arch Bridge, whose main span was the longest in the world when the picture was taken by an anonymous Detroit Photographic Company cameraman in 1908. A trolley and trailer are passing over it; other electric sightseeing railways ran up and down both sides of the Niagara River and Gorge, and by taking them, the 1909 Baedeker guidebook noted sharply, one could avoid the "extortionate charges and impertinent demeanour of the Niagara hackmen." So many excitements to distract those whom God had so recently joined together! The steamer *Maid of the Mist*, with its wet, thrilling ride; the Cave of the Winds, frightening enough to throw her into his brave arms; the "Natural Food Conservatory," where the canny Kelloggs were making their shredded wheat with waterpower. But it is easy to stray from reality at Niagara, for lovers or writers. What we want to say is that this is the most appealing photograph of the mighty cataract we have ever seen.

185

The Family

These are not, as one might think, characters out of *Wuthering Heights* or a particularly gloomy play by Eugene O'Neill. They are almost the folk memory of the American family of long ago, with a stern father, tight-lipped mother, three subdued and not very happy daughters, and a son or son-in-law of the same mien. Miscaptioned long ago in one of the library's many Brady collections of the Civil War era, the old print turns out to show an interesting American eccentric, John Minor Botts, and his family on the steps of their mansion in Culpeper County, Virginia. History touches this determined and often angry man in surprising ways. His lawyer father, Benjamin, had defended Aaron Burr; Botts Sr. and his wife both perished in the famous Richmond Theatre fire in 1811, when the boy was nine. John Minor Botts grew up to be a prominent Whig politician for thirty years, both in the Virginia legislature and the House of Representatives in Washington. His mind was firmly made up that the Democrats of the South were "conspirators" against the Union. He fought them over the Texas annexation and the war with Mexico. Though opposed himself to Abolition, he supported old John Quincy Adams in his fight against the "gag rule" in the House in Washington—the means whereby the Democrats suppressed all petitions from slaves or abolitionists. As a bitter enemy of secession, he was hated by the Confederate government and was thrust, as a token of their feelings, into Richmond's Negro jail by Jefferson Davis. Released, he bought the mansion in this picture, in a place so fought over that he could entertain at one time or another both Confederate and Union officers, denouncing secession to both sides. General J.E.B. Stuart once arrested him again, but he was released at once; by now southerners knew they were dealing with a man of principle. After the war Botts led the Virginia delegation to the "Convention of Southern Loyalists" at Philadelphia in 1866. But he lost his new position of influence when—again out of principle, not liking—he was one of those who signed the bail bond of Jefferson Davis. From the expressions on these faces, principle must at times have been a hard and cheerless master.

187

Suum Cuique

Man had his job, and at certain levels his private office, and there he worked "from sun to sun," or some reasonable approximation of that period, and the six-day week prevailed. His helpmeet's work, however, as the proverb went, was never done, except among those rich enough to afford help, in which case there was still a great deal of supervision, or at least fussing. There were many fewer packaged foods, and nearly all food was prepared, if not grown, at home. Baking, canning, needlework, laundry, and a thousand chores kept women constantly busy, without even reckoning with the care of the large families of the day. There is no actual connection, to be sure, between the dignified if unidentified gentleman at his desk, opposite, sent in 1906 by Underwood & Underwood as an unmounted stereograph, and the busy housewife below, peeling what seem to be apples in dress that is rather fancy for the task. The latter picture was made in 1902, where or for what reason we cannot imagine, by F. M. Steele. The photographer's caption reads simply, "Have One?"

The pieties of a sentimental and, at times, lachrymose age were the province of women. They were the steadiest church-goers, the managers of weddings and funerals, the principal audience for sorrowful poetry, the general keepers, in sum, of sacred flames. Below, in a stereograph for the feminine trade, is a kind of mourning piece, all fussy paper flowers and gauze, around a likeness of little Charlie Ross, a four-year-old Philadelphia child who was abducted in 1874 and never seen again—a sufficiently rare event in those days to stir widespread fear among parents everywhere. The scene opposite is a similar triumph in the mournful genre; a more woebegone tableau would be hard to imagine. There could not possibly have been a dry eye in the house when this sixteen-by-twenty-inch print was exhibited at a camera club in St. Louis.

A Man's World . . .

Men, it was widely suspected by women, were a rough and often uncouth lot, fond of fishing and hunting and always eager to get off by themselves and swap their unspeakable jokes. One of these, it is clear, has just been told in the photograph above; from his expression, it has even embarrassed the porter, who ought to have been used to traveling salesmen by now. For the date, 1905, and the close quarters in a Pullman sleeper, it is

an unusual action picture, although no doubt posed by the photographer, George R. Lawrence, called "Flashlight" Lawrence for his pioneer indoor work. As for the hunters in their canoe, at right, complete with dogs and a large buck, it would be hard to find a better composition on this subject today, even though the photograph was taken in 1890. It is one of a few oversize prints copyrighted by Seneca Ray Stoddard, the Adirondack specialist, who no doubt expected to sell a good many of them for framing. An expert canoeist himself, Stoddard and a friend paddled the entire distance from the mouth of the Hudson along the New England coast to the head of the Bay of Fundy in the 1880's. They covered a full twenty-one hundred miles during their ambitious journey, breaking the trip into five sections during as many August vacations.

It was an article of faith among women, at least in some circles, that only constant, prayerful attention can prevent the male of the species from sinking into total degradation. Unwatched, he will vanish into the pit, the fate of the untidy character in the anonymous photograph at the right, labeled very simply "Prosit!" His children, no doubt, have no shoes, and his wife is taking in washing. He is very clearly well past the first and fatal glass of beer—and past any possible attendance at the inspiring service in the stereograph below, made in 1899 by Strohmeyer and Wyman. Entitled "The Village Choir," it was, like so much other stereoscopic work in that era, probably intended to be funny, like the old souse. But one can never be entirely sure.

Ladies, as opposed to women in general—a delicate distinction in pre-Freudian times—did not belong to the PTA, or Planned Parenthood, or NOW (the National Organization of Women), none of which existed. They might join the Women's Christian Temperance Union or the women's auxiliary of almost any men's organization; they might even be members of a suffrage organization. The great organization to

belong to, however, was the Daughters of the American Revolution. Its motto was Home and Country, and it was interested in history (you had to prove a Revolutionary ancestor), patriotism, and education. Eventually everyone made fun of it for, among other things, foolishly denying the use of its hall to Marian Anderson in 1939. But the Daughters, to do them justice, provided services on Ellis Island, main-

tained two schools for poor children, and supported other worthy activities then and now. Here the Board of Management sits in full regalia in 1905, with the President General, Mrs. Charles Warren Fairbanks, in the chair. She was the wife of the then Vice-President of the United States, and it was no handicap for either of them that he had been born in a log cabin and was a Methodist, an Abolitionist, and a Republican.

198

The American male is, and has been for a long time, a great joiner. Whether for the pleasure of the company of his peers, for the satisfaction of "getting in," for the secret pleasures of keeping others out—or simply to get out of the house—he loves his club or his lodge or his bowling team. Of all these organizations nothing could be more florid or satisfying than those with vivid costumes and secret rites. Here, for example, are the officers of Mecca Temple of the Ancient Arabic Order of Nobles of the Mystic Shrine, posing in New York in 1895. We assume that the gentleman with the long dagger in the center is that year's grand and exalted potentate, Augustus W. Peters. The Shriners are an appendant order of Masonry who undertake such good works as maintaining (today) twenty-two hospitals for crippled children, but they are also the jolly extroverts and paraders of the huge fraternity. There were fifty-five thousand Shriners in 1900; membership has swollen to nearly a million in our times. Masonry, with its many rites and orders, its "commanderies" of Knights Templar, its "grottoes" of Veiled Prophets, and its "forests" of Tall Cedars of Lebanon, goes back to the Middle Ages. Over the centuries it has been viewed with alarm by the papacy, fascist and communist states, and (one supposes) families who wish that Dad would come home soon.

"I'll have to ask Momma" is the caption for this tense moment in a series of slides by Strohmeyer & Wyman. The question is popped, and we now await the next move—although one's attention does stray to the impossible furnishings.

IX. Pandora's Box: The Stereoscope

It is a leaf torn from the book of God's recording angel.

—Dr. Oliver Wendell Holmes
on the stereoscope, 1859

The stereoscopic viewer, with its twin lenses and its accompanying boxes of slides, reposed on the piano, or perhaps on the parlor table, and was as much a part of life and home entertainment as the omnipresent television set of today. It was a great aid to courtship, like the family album, but nowhere near so limited in subject matter. The most popular topic for the stereoscope was travel. Sold in sets by many manufacturers, the slides took you to the great fairs and expositions, to palaces and castles, to faraway Arabia or nearby Philadelphia. You crossed the continent, traveled in liners, saw the aftermath of floods and disasters, and rode along with the cavalry on the plains. And the stereoscope had a magic quality that even television lacks—the third dimension, the quality that so enraptured Dr. Holmes that he invented the improved slide holder that older readers may remember. Not long after the stereoscope was brought to America in 1850 it became the largest single market for photographers. The Library of Congress collection in this field is enormous; many pictures throughout this volume are reproduced from stereographs. All the pictures in this chapter, however, are taken from one variety, the so-called "comics," in which the stereoscope anticipates by something like a century the modern situation comedy. Staged with actors in preposterous settings, they deal in sure-fire subjects like the pains of courtship, the adjustments of newly-weds, the plight of spinsters, and the cute pranks of children imitating the adults. The producers went in heavily for Cupids, stuffed birds, and double exposures, and the humor, admittedly, tended to be a little heavy-handed. But as social history, even in these broad strokes of near-parody, it is wonderfully revealing.

This universal birth fable, laid "in olden times" by the Keystone View Company, shows a whole stereographic slide in its double form.

Some idea of the size of the stereograph business may be gained from this view, a stereo itself, of the Order Department of the Kilburn Company at Littleton, New Hampshire. Beginning with the neighboring White Mountains but soon extending his travels to the world, aptly named Benjamin West Kilburn himself photographed much of the firm's product, seen assembled in sets on the tables above. The stereoscope itself was invented in England and is based on the principle that each human eye sees any given scene as a slightly different image. The two images, when superimposed either by the brain or in the stereoscopic viewer, give us depth perception. A German-American photographer, Frederick Langenheim, saw the process in London, and with his brother William introduced it to America, first on glass slides and later on paper. They also invented the stereopticon, a kind of improved magic lantern which is often confused with the stereoscope. The Langenheims, Kilburns, and the firm of E. and H. T. Anthony were the big three of the industry in its early days. Their drummers were everywhere and, if we can believe the silly scene at right, were such Lotharios that they would steal a kiss from the housewife while her husband tried out the product. But somehow this embarrassed young salesman does not manage to look the part.

The lady painting Cupid is a stock comic character, known from antiquity right up through the Marx Brothers: the spinster panting for love. This photograph is from an original glass stereo negative and therefore not retouched by the manufacturer. He would have attended to Cupid's modesty and cropped the ceiling to hide the fact that this is a stage set.

Is the message of this scene thoroughly clear? Cupid is getting poor results through his stethoscope. Buying that an-kle-length string of beads for the lady has done very little for the suitor's cause—and Cupid will probably catch pneumonia.

In the simpler setting of the back stoop things are moving along more smoothly between the hired man and the maid.

This 1889 wheeze is entitled "Retouching Portraits" and is by the Littleton View Company of Littleton, New Hampshire.

This affecting moment is "Before Marriage," photographed in 1900 by the Whiting View Company of Cincinnati, Ohio.

The next view, of course, is "After Marriage." Whiting, who was a good prophet, called these his Twentieth Century Series.

The idea in stereo humor, it must be clear by now, was never to stray from stereotypes. Poor wallflower! Cruel men! The appalling furnishings of the rooms must have been what the publishers thought would strike a home audience as high-toned.

The picture at left betrays at the top that it is a setup—or "set"—but this crowded rowboat is real enough. It reflects the eternal and (to women) irritating truth that bachelors, no matter how superannuated, tend to make out much better than spinsters.

Marriage and its aftermath apparently never failed to get the laughs in the world of the stereoscope. This young bach-elor's pipe dreams are extensive. Which houri does he want? All three of them, perhaps? And what about the tiger skin?

"Her First Attempt" was confected in 1906 by the American Stereoscopic Company, one of the largest in the business. Af- ter pressing the pants wrong, the naive bride in such a series leaves you in stitches with her first cookies, all solid rock.

When they settled down with the viewer and a box of slides, folks of the Mauve Decade wanted to be reassured that men were just as bad as you suspected. Here one has been toying with his steno, and his wife has caught him red-handed.

Man's greatest problem, of course, is Drink: the set-piece scene was the saloon or the lodge meeting. In this older stereo- graph of the year 1875, the old soak has been detected as he tiptoes in. The hat and the guitar are particularly fine touches.

What brought down the house in collections of humorous stereographs was the children imitating their elders—even if it took a special uniform to organize this youthful version of that perennially sentimental scene, the soldier's farewell.

"Tea and Scandal," with a doll guest to share the tidbits, was made in 1874 by a Chicago photographer named Melander.

"Dressed for the Party," by the same Melander, pursues another famous theme with all the relentlessness of the genre.

"The New York & Chicago Limited Express," a bit more inventive, was made by the Fellows Company of Philadelphia.

In this untitled item the tots are playing bank, or budget, or panic, and they are using very large and very real paper money.

x. *Institutions*

This was an age when institutions and the men who ran them grandly looked their parts, from the senator, the judge, the parson, the soldier, and the professor right down to the cop on the beat and the fireman behind his snorting steeds. Some institutions were neglected, like the army, some were tottering a little, like the Protestant ascendancy, but others were enjoying a glorious dawn. Consider, for example, the splendid old scholar on the opposite page. He is Daniel Coit Gilman, first president of the University of California, then the first president of Johns Hopkins. When Hopkins, a wealthy man from Baltimore, left seven million dollars to found a true graduate university, three of the country's leading educators, Presidents Eliot of Harvard, Angell of Michigan, and White of Cornell, each wrote, unbidden, a letter recommending Gilman as its president. At Hopkins, he spent the money, not on buildings, but on collecting such brilliant faculty, visitors, and fellows as Thomas Huxley, Josiah Royce, John Dewey, Frederick Jackson Turner, Walter Hines Page, William Osler, and future President Woodrow Wilson. In an address on Gilman's retirement in 1901, Wilson said, ". . . you were the first to create and organize in America a university in which the discovery and dissemination of new truth were conceded a rank superior to mere instruction." Like few countries, America from the beginning was devoted to the ideal of universal education. But, of some three hundred forty supposed institutions of higher learning in the 1880's, James Bryce would concede that "not more than twelve" would fall within his definition of a university. In the "universities" of some of the southern and what he called "ruder Western states," faculties were small, averaging five or six. At one of these hopeful campuses Bryce met the president, whom, in a later telling of the encounter, he hid under the disguise of "Mr. Johnson." This eager man dilated at length about his grant from the legislature and the ambitious plans of "the faculty." Finally, his British visitor relates, "I asked of how many professors the faculty at present consisted. 'Well,' he answered, 'just at present the faculty is below its full strength, but it will soon be more numerous.' 'And at present?' I inquired. 'At present it consists of Mrs. Johnson and myself.' " In 1870 only four million children were attending elementary schools, taught in most cases by young girls passing time before marriage. There were only two hundred public high schools and fifty-two thousand college students, principally males. Harvard's collegiate faculty, largest in the country, numbered sixty-two.

Daniel Coit Gilman, recorded here in his academic robes by Frances Benjamin Johnston, went to school in his native Norwich, Connecticut, with Timothy Dwight, later president of Yale, and was in the same Yale class with Andrew D. White, first president of Cornell.

For the universities the years after the Civil War were times of ferment. Princeton, which had relied principally on students from the South, had been almost wiped out by the conflict; it had a small enrollment and very little money. In 1868 it called in a Scottish theologian and religious philosopher, James McCosh, fifty-six, to put things back together. In two decades he not only managed to make Princeton a fine place for Woodrow Wilson to be president of, but manged to reconcile his own arcane Scottish theology with the upstart notions of Darwin. He appears on the opposite page, strolling in a handsome campus setting after his retirement in 1888. Only a year after McCosh came to Princeton, Harvard installed Charles William Eliot, thirty-five, for what became a forty-year term. To the distress of traditionalists, Eliot was both a layman in religion and a crusader for educational change. He gave Harvard the radically new elective system, organized its pioneering School of Business Administration, and in 1873 appointed his remarkable cousin, Charles Eliot Norton (below, in a portrait by Purdy), to the first American university chair of fine arts. Polished, well-traveled, wealthy, friendly, a brilliant scholar and translator of Dante, an intimate of most of the literary notables of the age, he was a profound and broadening influence on thousands of Harvard men, the epitome of the man of letters as teacher and classroom "star."

Here, as it perhaps wished to be remembered, the Yale Class of 1873 seems to be meeting for an informal but outlandishly elongated photograph. Some of the young gentlemen are chatting, a few are reading, the rest are staring off into space. The boys average about twenty-two and a half years in age and include representatives from faraway parts of the country as well as New England. Of scholarship boys there were few. The picture, as a bit of study will reveal, is a composite, for which everyone has posed separately. Cutting out the individuals, assembling them into reasonably realistic groups and re-

photographing the result—not to mention doing it all in alphabetical order—must have been blinding, frustrating work. Such poses were a specialty of the firm of William Notman, the first great photographer of Canada, and his two sons. They even recorded "football games," assembling individual players against backdrops less realistic than the one below. The Notmans left an archive of some forty thousand items to McGill University, but their pictures circulated below the border because the subjects bought copies. Notman had at least three branch studios in American cities.

Higher education for women was still young and aspiring when these fine photographs were taken at the beginning of the twentieth century. The stereograph below, by C. H. Graves, shows Wellesley College girls enjoying the Hunnewell Arboretum in 1901, with the college buildings across the water in the background. The handsome, erect lady opposite, in a 1903 portrait by the Purdy Studio in Boston, is Mary Emma Woolley, who had recently been chosen president of Mount Holyoke, when she was only thirty-six. In her subsequent thirty-seven-year tenure of that office and in her many outside interests this lifelong spinster typified the social activism of a new breed of American woman. She was a Biblical scholar, the first woman to study (as an advanced-degree candidate) at Brown, an able speaker, a good administrator who soon doubled the size of Mount Holyoke and made it second only to Bryn Mawr as a producer of scholarly women. She hired professors of both sexes but was feminist enough to refuse to install a course in home economics. Outside the campus she fought against sweatshops, teachers' oaths, and secret societies, for disarmament and equal suffrage, attending so many different conferences that the trustees began to complain. When they appointed a man to succeed her she was so bitter—on principle, her friends said—that she never set foot again on the campus.

The bottom of the educational pyramid, if only because it was so wide, was the public elementary school—universal free education for "every class and rank of people," as John Adams once demanded. We would have no illiterate peasantry, no ignorant city proletariat. It was only in the late nineteenth century, however, that America began to attain the dream. In 1870, in the days of McGuffey's readers and the birch rod, only some 6,870,000 children were enrolled in the public schools; by 1900 there were 15,500,000. Pressed by progressive ideas, the schools had become almost unrecognizable. Those in Washington, D.C., in fact, were so pleased with themselves that Frances Benjamin Johnston was called on to document their activities. Exercise, hygiene, science, and practical knowledge had been added to the old curriculum, and the wonderful sample scene below shows students of the Fifth Division at work learning measurement.

This encouraging scene, at least from a dental standpoint, cropped up in a file of pictures sent in 1919 to the Library of Congress by the Tennessee Coal, Iron & Railroad Company, which maintained schools for its employees' children at its Fairfield, Alabama, plant. The caption reads "White Tooth-brush Drill," which is, unfortunately, not the opposite of "Pink Toothbrush Drill," but indicates that this was the company's school for white children in segregated Alabama. A companion photograph shows the black students at their school, every one of them happily waving a small American flag. The company, so proud of its school system, had been merged in 1907 into the giant United States Steel Corporation.

The National Game

No outdoor sport ever attained such standing in America as baseball—although it was unknown in really recognizable form before the Civil War. Thereafter professional baseball quickly became an institution, and the game flourished in every sandlot by the time the self-conscious pair of Princeton men at left took their stances in 1901—although in college circles football teams enjoyed greater cachet, especially in the Ivy League. Perhaps that was because football satisfied the national blood lust; President Eliot of Harvard tried to rule it off the campus to stop the mayhem, to the disgust of President Theodore Roosevelt, a Harvard man. Baseball required skill rather than brute force, and even girls took it up. In the immortal scene below, according to the National Photographic Company caption, Virginia Smoot of Washington's Columbia Junior High is being tagged out at third by Mabel Harvey of the McFarland School. What the girls lack in form they are making up in enthusiasm. Virginia is going to make a three-point landing, we fear, and take Mabel with her.

Until Andy Carnegie bestowed public libraries on what sometimes seemed every crossroads, these institutions were not numerous. To serve one was a distinction—and it still is today. Here, looking patrician and deadly serious, is the Board of Trustees of the Boston Public Library, meeting to discuss which new books to purchase and to consider the new library building just designed for them by the noted New York City architectural firm of McKim, Mead and White. From the left, the trustees are Henry W. Haynes, a lawyer, archaeologist, and professor of classics; Frederick Prince, a former mayor of Boston; Chairman Samuel A. B. Abbott, the librarian himself, who ran the library for many years and sits on an appropriately higher chair; the Reverend William R. Richards, a prominent Boston clergyman; and Phineas Pierce, whose bartender's mustache belies his expertise as the library's financial adviser. Attention must be invited to the high button shoes, the gold watch chains, and the tubular trousers. Pressing a seam into them was, in 1894 when this majestic quintet sat for posterity, a "Johnny-boy" notion, to be eschewed at all costs by gentlemen.

226

These two august countenances presided over the Supreme Court of the United States during all the long years between 1888 and 1921—although it is doubtful whether very many readers, even lawyers, will recognize them or recall their names. The seat at the very apex of the huge, babbling American legal pyramid—with its great and unique power of judicial review—is rarely given to great lawyers like Daniel Webster or Joseph Choate, or to legal philosophers like Oliver Wendell Holmes, Louis Brandeis, or Learned Hand. It is offered to middling men like these. On the facing page is Melville Weston Fuller, born in Maine, later a dull but able Chicago lawyer. President Cleveland made him Chief Justice in 1888, and in 1894 appointed the heavyset Louisiana politician above, Edward Douglass White, as an associate justice. When Fuller died in 1910, Taft nominated White for Chief Justice. Both these magistrates had "read law" in the old-fashioned way, both were "deserving Democrats" as well; but both rose to their responsibilities.

Guardians of the Law

At the other end of the legal establishment from the judges on the preceding pages, photographs from the turn of the century bring us the police, looking exactly as one would expect them to: like Keystone Kops. The carefully set-up New York scenes on these pages are examples of early "feature" or documentary work by photographers responding to the demands of the press. The officers tend to the portly, they employ new devices like the telephone, and they wear white gloves. There is, we must add, nothing new about crime waves in big cities. Under the title of "Lawless New York," for example, *Harper's Weekly* for December 19, 1908, reported with horror that by the most conservative estimates (those of the police) there had been 757 homicides in the first nine months of the year, with 93.3 per cent of the suspects sooner or later set free to continue the mayhem. What with holdups, bombings, stabbings, bloody family quarrels, gang wars, and what *Harper's* called "Black Hand outrages," these helmeted officers had full days ahead of them.

The scenes exhibited here, a little fuzzy because taken from motion-picture film, demonstrate that there is nothing new about *Kojak* or America's fascination with the war between crime and the law. They are excerpted from *The Life of an American Policeman*, a movie documentary of a sort, showing the nickelodeon audience that the cop might have his foibles at the fruit stand but he was a loyal friend of children, the distressed, and his buddies. Overtaxing belief a bit, it also purports to show him on a bicycle overhauling the hit-and-run driver of a speeding touring car. In the early days of the movies a few stills like these would be accepted for copyright in lieu of a copy of the film itself. But, aside from such stills, the Library of Congress now possesses over fifty thousand actual films, including early ones from the pioneer Edison Laboratories, primitive comedies and documentaries, and collections on Mary Pickford and William S. Hart.

1. *The day shift hits the pavement.*

2. *What's an apple between friends?*

3. *A gunman shoots down a patrolman.*

4. *Other cops rush to his assistance . . .*

5. . . . and the "perpetrator" is subdued.

6. At a pier, a woman is rescued.

7. She receives first aid on the spot.

8. Elsewhere a child is saved from a car.

9. The guilty motorist is pursued . . .

10. and nabbed by the bicycle police.

233

Last Run

Hooves clattering on the pavement and heads tossing, the fire horses race by, pulling a steam pumper, and every man stops to watch. Small boys, if not restrained, will run after the apparatus until exhausted. Those who know the alarm signal codes will sagely explain where the fire must be. In this case, whether the onlookers knew it or not, photographer Herbert E. French was recording the final run, in 1925, of the District of Columbia's last three fire horses, Barney, Gene, and Tom, who were then retired to a farm outside the city. In small towns and big cities alike, in the decades before this picture was taken, fire was the most dreaded, yet most dramatic event, and the fireman a most satisfactory hero. Furthermore, fire fighters were an important part of political and social life. To get into a proud and stylish volunteer hose company was difficult; leading citizens and businessmen were counted in the crews that fell into harness themselves and pulled by their own leg power the old-time hand pumpers. Nine mayors of New York owed their election, in part at least, to the support of fellow firemen. It was a rowdy business at times, with the belligerent rival companies more intent on beating their fellows, or beating them up, than on extinguishing a blaze. The coming of professionals, and of horse-drawn equipment, was a relief to the insurance companies—yet, ironically, as much a source of sadness and nostalgia to fire buffs as the arrival, decades later, of the motorized equipment that replaced chargers like the ones shown here.

235

The postal empire over which deserving Democrats and Republicans alternately presided ranged from the outpost above, in Searsburg, Vermont, to a great fortress in New York City. By frugal New England standards, Searsburg's was a sensible structure, a recycled packing box with a clever arrangement of strings to summon the postmaster from his garden patch, farther up the hill. It had wash-up facilities, and a sunny reading area for catalogue study. New York's, as expensive as might be expected, cost ten million dollars when it went up in 1875, a marvel of neo-Renaissance or high General Grant style, a Pelion of mansard on an Ossa of columns and pilasters, a temple in which it must have seemed almost a

sacrilege to mail a penny postcard. Up to the left in J. S. Johnston's 1894 photograph runs Broadway. A horse car waits to head up Park Row to the right, and one of the new electric cars, with its trailer, prepares to run around a loop. The handsome building came down in 1939—which might have been expected in light of the poor economic performance of the post office from its very birth two hundred years ago. The British mails in America ceased functioning in December, 1775; by 1779 postal rates under the free and independent Continental Congress were twenty times as high. Inflation, to be sure, played some role in the price rise, and is still assisting us vigorously. The advantages of throwing off colonial yokes cannot be overstressed.

Military Men

"Half a mile of troops," reads the caption of this stereograph; it shows the 15th United States Cavalry on a three-hundred-mile march through southern Vermont around 1905, but is otherwise unlocated. From the interurban railway we might guess at Brattleboro. The military as an institution occupied between wars a dubious place in American life. The "thirst for military glory" that Edward Gibbon found so distressing in Rome had not become an addiction—useful as that glory might be at the polls after America's wars. The Regular Army on the eve of World War I numbered only 95,000— less than a fourth the size of Turkey's. Most people felt that soldiering was such an easy business that the militia, springing to arms in the tradition of the minuteman, would be able to take care of any trouble. On the other hand, as this rural scene clearly testifies, everybody loved a parade.

OVERLEAF: The cavalry, with its pounding hooves and fluttering guidons, was the most romantic part of the Army, especially to generations reared on "Sheridan's Ride" and "The Charge of the Light Brigade." In the words of a famous cartoon in *Punch*, it lent "tone to what would otherwise be a vulgar brawl," but it suffered from two problems. In the age of the machine gun it was obsolete. And it was difficult to work up things to do with it between charges. This scene shows one solution found in 1900 by Company F of the 6th Cavalry. The men have mounted and surrounded a tree called "The Fallen Monarch" in the Mariposa Big Tree Grove in Yosemite, and are having their picture taken by the South Pacific Company. The tree is vanquished and will give Company F no more trouble.

239

On the sunny afternoon of September 28, 1910, veterans of the 143rd Pennsylvania Infantry and some of their womenfolk gathered by their own monument on the battlefield of Gettysburg. Wind ruffles their gray hair and keeps a flag snapping while the Battlefield Photo Company's operative exposes group picture No. 2261 (and later takes orders for prints). It is forty-seven years

since the 143rd, led by Colonel Edmund L. Dana, was part of Major General Abner Doubleday's First Army Corps in the biggest, most furious battle—not to mention the most decisive—ever fought in the United States. Their brigade, the 2nd, was part of the 3rd Division, consisting of three Pennsylvania outfits. It lost 84 killed, 462 wounded, and 306 missing.

With some justice, republics fear professional soldiers, the images of Rome's Praetorian Guard and the Prussian officer corps always in their mind. The United States Military Academy at West Point goes back to 1802 and the conviction of Washington, Hamilton, and Henry Knox that we could not place our entire reliance in time of war on militia generals and politicians in uniform. It was not until 1845, however, that the United States got a naval academy, and that unwillingly. The sea, in its mysterious way, was supposed to produce great captains out of cabin boys—Nelson and Paul Jones, for example. Admiral Tromp went to sea at eight, Farragut at nine, David Dixon Porter at thirteen. The wonderful picture at top right of exercise at West Point was taken in 1889 by Seneca R. Stoddard, the photographer of the Adirondacks, and labeled "embryo cavalry"; we can identify no one. The picture below, made by Frances Benjamin Johnston in 1901, shows members of the Class of 1902 at Annapolis; they are sitting on the Second Class Bench, a special privilege, or "rate," of their class in the stratified Naval Academy. In front of the Tripoli Monument sits James O. Richardson, oldest man in his class. Despite the promotion system, loaded against older midshipmen, he made four-star rank and, in 1940 and early 1941, Commander in Chief of the United States Fleet. He was removed after disagreeing with the administration's plan to keep the Pacific fleet at Pearl Harbor.

244

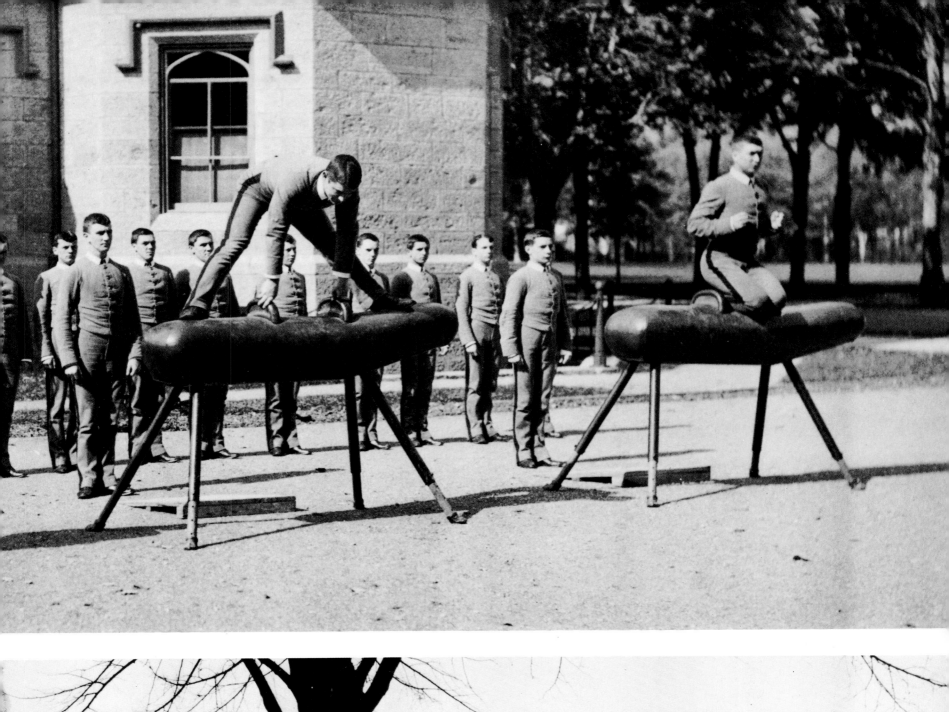

Despite every urging of religion, philosophy, and experience, war always seems to call to man from a level too deep for change. Turn-of-the-century America, for all the disapproving voices, was fascinated by two recent conflicts—nothing much at bloodletting by modern standards but full of derring-do. One was our own martial exercise with Spain, the other Britain's South African War. War is good theater, as every great poet and dramatist has realized and as the two stereographs at left bear witness. They show re-enactments staged daily at the St. Louis world's fair of 1904—battleships at Santiago de Cuba, above, and some kind of battle in South Africa, below; the old captions are bare-bones affairs. Sentiment in the United States ran heavily in favor of the brave, resourceful, and down-to-earth Boers, whose struggle against big British armies reminded us of our own revolution. As for the blacks—who have since replaced the Boers in popular favor—no one worried about "natives" at all in those days, except as colorful types to be discovered, photographed, and converted into Baptists.

One aspect of the Spanish-American War that charmed the sentimental was the fact that a few graying veterans of the Union and Confederate armies, now in their fifties and sixties, were fighting in it side by side. In the 1898 patriotic extravaganza at right, officers in blue and gray symbolically shake hands, brought together by pretty little Cuba, whose chains are rent asunder. The author was a Union veteran who had received the Congressional Medal of Honor, Captain Fritz W. Guerin of St. Louis, winner of many photographic awards in an earlier and simpler day. Several large shelves at the library sag under a collection of Guerin's "art studies" and giant prints of his earnest tableaux, most of them peopled with lightly clad but heavily symbolic female models.

Keeping Busy

It is December, 1918, the war is over, and you, commanding officer at Camp Gordon in Atlanta, Georgia, have thousands of men, not to mention nurses, twiddling their thumbs or engaged in what a later age would call Mickey Mouse. But then relief appears in the resourceful person of Arthur S. Mole, photographer, of the Chicago firm of Mole & Thomas. Mr. Mole has a seventy-five-foot ladder and a brilliant, time-consuming idea. He will tape off your parade ground in an enormous pattern and then arrange 12,500 officers and men to represent the American eagle, with white-uniformed nurses and men in skivvy shirts or long underwear to help emphasize the design. In an interesting exercise in reverse perspective, requiring thousands in the background and mere scores in the foreground, the photographer-impresario climbs his ladder, shouts a good deal, and makes the picture shown here. The exercise is politically safe, because Mole has already reproduced by the same methods the United States shield at Camp Custer in Battle Creek, Michigan (30,000 men), Old Glory at the Great Lakes Naval Station (10,000 men), and the Liberty Bell at Camp Dix, New Jersey (25,000 men). He has even done a profile likeness of President Wilson with 21,000 doughboys at Camp Sherman, Ohio, and there have been no impertinent questions in the press about what it costs to keep thousands of men standing around for hours at taxpayers' expense. In fact, a leather-bound set of these extraordinary photographs was presented by Mole to Secretary of the Navy Josephus Daniels. His heirs passed them on to the Library of Congress. The trouble with armies and navies is not how to recruit and arm them, as any veteran knows. It's what to do with them next.

248

XI. Causes

Vainly do we preach the blessings of temperance to human beings cradled in hunger and suffering at intervals the agonies of famine; idly do we commend intellectual culture to those whose minds are daily racked with the dark problem, "How shall we procure food for the morrow?"

—Horace Greeley

From the very beginning, the little colonies along the eastern seaboard and the aspiring republic they presently set up represented an almost religious ideal. America was a land of infinite possibilities, both material and spiritual. It is all there in "America the Beautiful," from the alabaster cities to the amber waves of grain: "America! America! God mend thine every flaw,/Confirm thy soul in self-control,/Thy liberty in law! . . ./And crown thy good with brotherhood,/From sea to shining sea!" To a more cynical age, which has lived to see limits finally set to its dreams, the flaw-menders, the crusaders of earlier times, may seem quaint and a little pompous. But looking into the faces of the reformers in this chapter, one finds a common quality, which is optimism. They share a conviction that the cause will triumph, and it is a conviction in many cases justified. Some causes fail, like prohibition or spiritualism—although they still have grim adherents. Some are won, like abolitionism. Some, like "General" Coxey's crusade for road-building, relief work, and cheap money, succeed beyond anyone's dreams. And brotherhood is still a bit around the corner. America had many peacetime marchers between the Civil War and World War I, as the picture files attest; the problem, of course, was the differing drums. Most of the nineteenth century's political battles and carpetbagsful of its causes converge in the earnest, hard-working, disheveled figure of Horace Greeley, left, the great editor of the New York *Tribune*. He fought slavery but was vacillating in his support of Lincoln. He was for total abstinence, protective tariffs, spiritualism, the workingman, and the Homestead Act; he was against monopoly, capital punishment, woman suffrage, theaters, and easy divorce. No man's opinions were more widely read, for the *Tribune*'s various daily and weekly editions reached all over the country. Our picture shows him, worn out at about sixty, when he was undertaking a disastrous campaign for the presidency against U. S. Grant, pledging to shake hands again with the South "across the bloody chasm." As he went down in defeat, Greeley lost his wife, his paper, and his mind. The old reformer died three weeks after the election—mourned by his whole country, friends and enemies alike.

Even late in life Horace Greeley retained the look of an elderly baby who has not quite managed to get his clothes on right. He was fired from an early typesetting job on the New York *Evening Post* by a boss who wanted only "decent-*looking* men in the office." His education ended at fourteen, but he spent a lifetime educating others.

Nineteenth-century Boston, according to Oliver Wendell Holmes, was "the thinking center of the continent." The city also served as America's conscience; there, high in their moral aerie, an extraordinary group of reformers shaped events by sheer weight of personality. Julia Ward Howe stood in the front of their ranks for most of her long life, despite the protests of her husband, Samuel Gridley Howe—himself a tireless reformer. In 1862 she worked the rough lyrics of "John Brown's Body" into the great Union anthem "The Battle Hymn of the Republic." The fame thus gained gave weight to her endorsement of various worthy causes, among them abolition, prison reform, and women's rights.

Thomas Wentworth Higginson, another Brahmin friend of the slave, carried his convictions into the field during the Civil War. Many abolitionists were pacifists, but Higginson would have none of that—the religious group he headed had earned its nickname of the "Jerusalem wildcats"—and when the war broke out he left the ministry to take command of the first black regiment in the Union army. Wounded, he returned home in 1864 and devoted the rest of his life to an array of good works. Toward the end of his days, he genially announced that he felt much like a horse "which had never won a race, but which was prized as having gained a second place in more races than any other horse in America."

Surrounded by his poison squad, Old Borax stands on the steps of the Bureau of Chemistry offices in Washington, D.C., in 1899, looking every bit the hardy campaigner that he was. Dr. Harvey Wiley drew his nickname from his first experiments on food adulterants, in which he attempted to determine if the borax then used to preserve butter had harmful side effects. It did, as he found out by feeding the substance to the men of his newly recruited "poison squad." After that, he went on to offer his troops a diet of saltpeter, benzoates, formaldehyde, copper sulfate, and all the other chemicals the packing houses liked to use. These experiments, said Wiley, made his laboratory "the most highly advertised boarding-house in the world," and he used the publicity to push through, in 1906, the first Pure Food and Drug Law—despite the carping of the New York *Sun* that he had no right to act as the "chief janitor and policeman of people's insides."

Though Dwight L. Moody never attempted to get himself ordained, he was a superb evangelist, a tough old Bible-thumper who was never sentimental about his Maker and who wasn't afraid to spread His word in some pretty grim places. Lightly educated though he was, young Moody became a highly successful businessman after he moved from Boston to Chicago in 1856. Three years later, at the age of twenty-three, he was pulling in upward of five thousand dollars a year. But he felt the call and, in 1860, he left business entirely to become an unsalaried independent city missionary. A forceful and popular speaker, he drummed up the funds for a nondenominational church and worked hard for the Y.M.C.A., a duty that took him into alleys like this one where, photographed in 1877, he stands among urchins whose toughness is indicated by their names: Butcher Kilroy, Red Eye, Indian, Rag-breeches Cadet, and Madden the Butcher.

Coxey's Army

Jacob Sechler Coxey's "petition in boots" started out from Massillon, Ohio, a hundred strong on a gray, snowy Easter Sunday in the depression year of 1894. The ragged army—an amalgam of unemployed artisans, hoboes, and eccentrics—was bound for Washington, where it would present Congress with two bills designed by Coxey to provide jobs for all who wanted them. The first, the Good Roads Bill, called on the Treasury to issue five hundred million dollars to improve country roads; the second gave state and city governments the right to issue bonds for local improvements, to be carried out by men working an eight-hour day. The man who propounded these schemes was a well-to-do quarry owner with strong populist sympathies. Himself a retiring man, Coxey recruited a picturesque blowhard named Carl Browne to ballyhoo the March; Browne is shown in the photograph opposite, which was taken by the Washington firm of J. F. Jarvis, riding Coxey's seven-thousand-dollar stallion. The well-organized march picked up recruits along the way; the ranks had swollen to two hundred when the army crossed into Pennsylvania. Coxey was proud of his men's discipline. Though they marched past hundreds of hen houses, he said, "You cannot find so much as a chicken feather among my men." Some towns proved sympathetic and fed the army; in others, the men were met at the county line by sheriffs like the quintessential small-town bull above. His picture comes from the scrapbook of Ray Stannard Baker, a reporter who accompanied the march and whose cool, balanced accounts did much to offset the hysterical press the crusade tended to generate. On May 1, Coxey led four hundred and fifty followers to the steps of the Capitol—where he was promptly arrested and jailed for walking on the grass. The bills never passed. Coxey went home to spend the rest of his days running for various offices, ranging from local minor factotum to President of the United States. But he only succeeded once; between 1931 and 1933 he served as mayor of Massillon.

Agony in Lawrence

"It is the first strike I ever saw which sang," wrote Ray Stannard Baker from the midst of a struggle far grimmer than Coxey's quixotic, orderly march of nearly twenty years earlier. "I shall not soon forget the curious lift, the strange sudden fire of the mingled nationalities at the strike meetings when they broke into the universal language of song." Baker should not have been surprised to hear the strikers singing in the cold winter streets of Lawrence, Massachusetts, for the Industrial Workers of the World was a singing union, and had been from the beginning. Founded in 1905, the IWW, whose members were nicknamed wobblies, sought to organize the people that Sam Gompers and the educated artisans of the AFL wouldn't touch—the migratory workers, the millhands, the nation's whole great pool of unskilled labor. The leaders realized that it was easier to put across their message in songs than in tracts, and by 1913 their songbook was being printed in batches of fifty thousand. A year before that, the huge American Woolen Company at Lawrence had cut its wages,

and twenty-five thousand workers walked away from their jobs. They petitioned the IWW, then at the peak of its power, and the union sent in organizers, among them Joseph J. Ettor, who counseled solidarity and, above all, peace. "They cannot weave cloth with bayonets," he said. "By all means make this strike as peaceful as possible . . ., all the blood spilled will be your blood. . . . Violence necessarily means the loss of the strike." Nevertheless, William Wood, the president of the company, declared "There is no strike at Lawrence, just mob rule." (He had to temper his indignant tone a bit later when he was indicted for planting dynamite in an attempt to brand the

strikers as terrorists.) The governor ordered out the militia—shown with bayonets in the Bain photograph at left—but the strike went on. As things got worse, the workers sent their children to stay in other towns. In New York they marched down Fifth Avenue, below, bearing placards—a demonstration so effective that Lawrence authorities forbade any more children to leave the city. When a hundred and fifty tried to go, policemen lit into them with clubs. That scrap turned the tide; afterward, nearly everyone sided with the workers. On March 12, sixty-three days after the strike began, the company gave in. Two weeks after that, the children came home.

The Anarchist

"The Anarchist," said President Theodore Roosevelt, "is the enemy of humanity, the enemy of mankind, and his is a deeper degree of criminality than any other." The depraved creature he described and the smooth-faced, awkward youth shown above are one and the same. He is Alexander Berkman, the lover of Emma Goldman—another enemy of mankind—and the would-be assassin of the industrialist Henry Clay

Frick. Born in Vilna, then part of Russia, in 1870, Berkman emigrated to America in 1887 and almost immediately became active in New York's radical labor groups. He was living with his fellow immigrant Emma Goldman when they got word of the Homestead steel strike in Pennsylvania. The worst labor clash of its era, the 1892 strike left thirteen dead after a pitched battle fought between the strikers and Pinkertons hired by

Frick. Seeking vengeance, Berkman went to Homestead—Goldman would have joined him, but they couldn't scrape up her train fare—burst into Frick's office, and there shot and stabbed him. This "propaganda of the deed," as Berkman called it, was a costly gesture both for him and for his cause. Public opinion, which had been running heavily against Frick, immediately reversed itself: Frick became a fine American and a martyr to godless anarchy. Tried without benefit of legal counsel, Berkman spent fourteen years in jail for a crime which, according to Pennsylvania law, carried a sentence of no more than seven. He emerged with his beliefs unshaken, and gave tongue to them forcefully and often. In the 1908 Bain photograph above, the unrepentant anarchist addresses a group of wobblies in New York's Union Square.

Even in the dangerous climate of an incipient world war, Berkman refused to back off from his radical politics. In the Bain Service's 1914 photograph at right, he strides confidently along with a young woman named Helen Harris, looking more plutocratic than anarchistic in his neatly creased trousers and starched collar. Almost alone among labor figures, Emma Goldman had stayed loyal to him following his attempt on Frick's life, and the two remained close friends for years—despite anything that may have been going on with Miss Harris. As energetic a proselytizer as Berkman, Goldman was not a particularly original thinker, but she could put across her views from the podium with wit, vigor, and clarity. At left, she rides with Berkman (who is wearing the straw hat) in an open streetcar. Above her head, Uncle Sam waves an admonitory finger from James Montgomery Flagg's famous recruiting poster; this is 1917, America has entered World War I, and Berkman and Goldman do not have much time left in the States. Both opposed the war violently—a stand that also brought the IWW to grief—and in the summer of 1917 were found guilty of conspiracy to obstruct the operation of the selective service law and thrown into jail. Two years later, they were deported to Russia, thanks largely to the efforts of young J. Edgar Hoover, then head of the Justice Department's General Intelligence Division. It is some index of Goldman's power that nearly twenty years later he still regarded her deportation as his salient achievement.

Evangeline Booth, above, the "White Angel of the Slums," shelters two appealing waifs who are very different from Dwight Moody's street-wise kids. Despite this cloying 1907 composition, Booth was a tough-minded fighter. She put in her time on city street corners under the banner of the Salvation Army, which had been founded by her father William Booth in 1857. Like all good monarchies, the Army kept important things within the family, and Evangeline survived a good deal of bitter internecine squabbling to become its fourth general.

Under the auspices of the Bide-a-Wee home for animals, a spotless matron sees to it that horses are fitted out with sun hats—not, perhaps, so sweeping a cause as the freeing of proles or the saving of souls, but one doubtless appreciated by the patient beasts on the hot New York streets of August, 1907. Founded in 1903, Bide-A-Wee still offers shelter to homeless animals and administers two immaculate pet cemeteries on Long Island. It is impossible to say how far the hats-for-horses program got, but within a few years enterprises like the one behind the team in the picture would render the cause obsolete.

The Marchers

Dealing as it did with ancient and perennially charged issues, woman suffrage was among the oldest and most briskly contested of all causes. But the long fight is almost over for the women in this faintly surrealistic Bain photograph of November 9, 1912. They have posed on the roof of a New York building prior to joining twenty thousand of their sisters in a huge demonstration. The globes they brandish are lanterns that, come nightfall, will turn Fifth Avenue into what the New York *Times* called "a rolling stream of fiery lava." The strides their cause had made were reflected in the *Times*'s account of the event, which is altogether mellow and full of approbation: "As for the parade itself, it was a line, miles long, of well-dressed, intelligent women, deeply concerned in the cause they are fighting for." If there was a bad moment, it came when a man "behind an odor of alcohol" called out that the men in the demonstration "have to march or else their wives will beat them." But nobody was taking such slanders seriously anymore, and women secured the vote in time to help put Warren G. Harding in the White House.

XII. *Lively Artists*

Mark Twain always had a genuine
passion for billiards. He could play all
night. He would stay till the last man
gave out from sheer weariness; then
he would go on knocking the balls about
alone. He liked to invent new games
and new rules for old games, often inventing
a rule on the spur of the moment
to fit some particular shot. . . .
    —Albert Bigelow Paine, on the
    room where Twain did his writing

Like great banks of clouds, some gray, some fluffy, some only wispy, literary and artistic reputations glide by over the period of this book. As the nineteenth century drew to a close, the majestic array of Emerson, Hawthorne, Longfellow, Bryant, and Whittier dissolved. Historians who were read for pleasure—Parkman, Prescott, Bancroft—and poets who were memorized gave way to great thunderheads of philosophers: James, Spencer, Sumner, Dewey. The stern portraits that once adorned schoolroom walls now fill library files. In painting, new reputations were forming—Eakins, Ryder, Homer—departing from European models, although ordinary people's walls, like as not, were hung with sentimental, heroic, humorous, or improving lithographs of Currier & Ives. Sculpture, in the works of Saint-Gaudens, Daniel Chester French, and George Grey Barnard, had reached a kind of peak. Realistic, powerful, often patriotic in theme, it was all too often judged mainly on size—in which feature such art reached some kind of apogee in the 1920's when, with the on-site blessing of no less a student of art than Calvin Coolidge, the tempestuous Gutzon Borglum began blasting out his monumental row of presidential faces from the rock of Mount Rushmore, South Dakota. He appears below, checking up on George Washington's nose. The new writers who replaced the New England ascendancy came mainly out of journalism and its concern with real people, and of this coinage Mark Twain was undeniably the greatest, a humorist with a deep strain of pessimism in his soul. His *Huckleberry Finn* outraged respectable people: "If Mr. Clemens cannot think of something better to tell our pure-minded lads and lasses, he had best stop writing for them," snapped Louisa May Alcott. (Half a century later, Ernest Hemingway would say that all modern American literature came from that book.) Twain clearly liked being photographed for his public, and the stereograph at left catches him hamming a little in his workroom, which he shared with a billiard table, a useful aid to concentration.

Twain loved being photographed, loved his fine house in Hartford, Connecticut, and did his writing in his billiard room, opposite. At the right, Gutzon Borglum and one of his team of mountain-carvers dangle from the scaffolding.

What makes an artist to begin with and what makes some artists great and others merely good are doubtless matters of argument. But what brought aspiring painters to the growing bohemias of turn-of-the-century American cities must have been a mental image of something like this—the garret, the model, the free, romantic life. The photograph, a fine composition in its own right, was taken by Frances Benjamin Johnston in the studio of George Gibbs, a Philadelphia painter and illustrator. Beside him stands his friend and fellow student at the Corcoran School of Art in Washington, Mills Thompson, who had worked on the decoration of the Library of Congress building in 1896 and was later art editor of the *Saturday Evening Post*. Behind Thompson is a parlor stove and over Gibbs's head a gaslight fixture; they are as much tokens of the 1890's as the Oriental rug and the gentlemen's business dress. But the posture of the artist (and of the friendly critic) is eternal, and the beauty of the unidentified subject is both ineffable and compelling.

271

This carefully arranged art class was photographed sometime around 1890 by Frances Benjamin Johnston, but—as is unfortunately true of thousands of her pictures bestowed on the Library of Congress—there is no further information as to what this daring group was, or where it met, or who the perfectly cast instructor may have been. Despite the shield that can be lowered to hide him, the model is almost nude, and this in a day when Anthony Comstock was riding high, and his book, *Morals Versus Art*, barely off the press. "Nude paintings and statues," he wrote, "are the decoration of infamous resorts, and the law-abiding American will never admit them to the sacred confines of his home."

The actual number of young people who have developed a lifelong aversion to art by being told how to appreciate it en masse, in foot-weary groups like this, has not been uncovered, so far as we know, by data-thirsty educators. This group, with just five males visible among the dainty straw hats, was recorded some years after the picture opposite, also by Miss Johnston. The students, from Washington's Central High School, are visiting a gallery. It is unlikely that they were shown any impressionists or any improper modern paintings; acceptable taste was locked into French academic works, the kind of thing one might have seen at the World's Columbian Exposition in 1893. After visiting it, the expert J. P. Morgan coldly remarked that the French exhibit must have been selected by a committee of chambermaids.

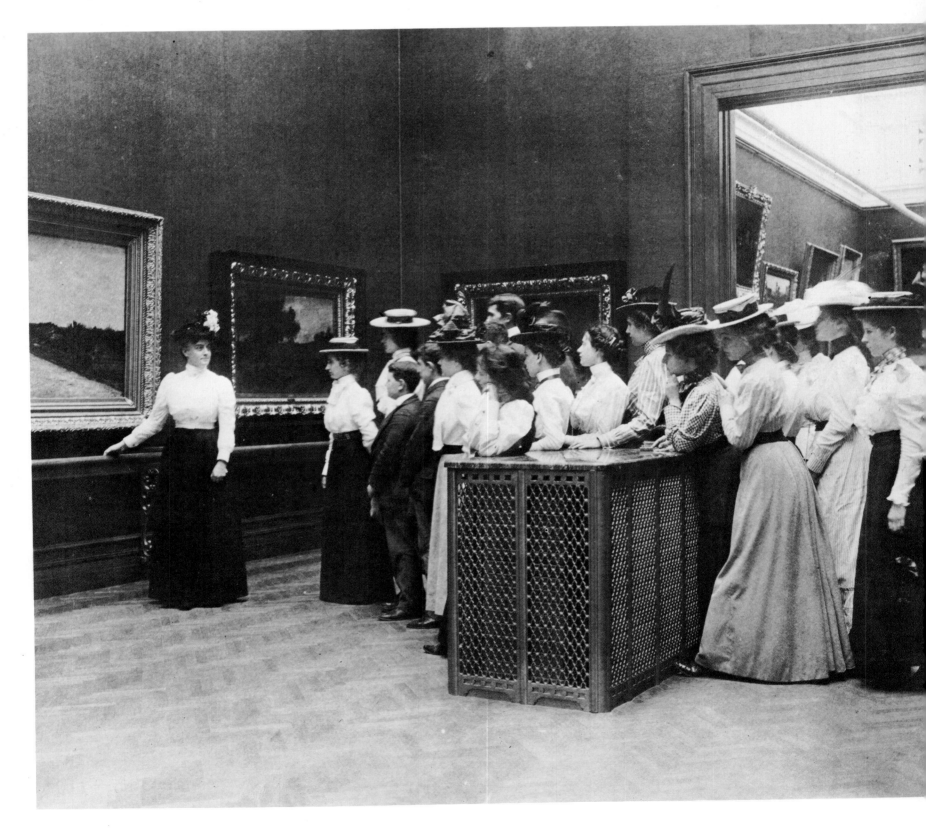

The Power of the Illustrators

In the closing years of the nineteenth century the three artists and illustrators shown here—whom few will recognize by their faces—enjoyed the kind of influence over thought and manners that has been wielded in modern times by motion pictures and television. The kindly old gentleman at the right, in a 1902 portrait by Pirie MacDonald, is the brilliant and savage caricaturist Thomas Nast, who more than any other single person destroyed the notorious Boss Tweed, the corrupt leader of Tammany Hall. When Tweed fled from justice and an outraged public to seek safety in Spain, it was a Nast cartoon that made him recognizable even there and brought him back to jail in America. Tweed's famous comment was that he didn't much mind what the papers wrote about him, since his constituents couldn't read anyway, but they could look at "those damn pictures." Nast also created the symbols of the parties—the Democratic donkey and the Republican elephant—and, loving children, he invented the fat, jolly Santa Claus figure that is still with us.

Howard Pyle, formally posed at left by Frances Benjamin Johnston, had little formal artistic training but became an enormously successful artist in many media, and the teacher of new young artists as able as N. C. Wyeth. His main fame rests, however, on the great children's tales he wrote or retold and then superbly illustrated, sometimes in a medieval pen-and-ink style, later on in color. With the possible exception of his pirate series, the tale best remembered today by several generations of ex-children was *The Merry Adventures of Robin Hood*, done in 1883. Even the great William Morris, who scorned American art, found plenty of praise for it.

Charles Dana Gibson was well born, and as clean-shaven, broad-shouldered, and square-jawed as any of his heroes—a set of virtues emphasized by Pirie MacDonald's 1903 portrait at right. In *Our Times* Frank Sullivan wrote that he "could express more with a single line of black on white than any other artist of his generation." His "Gibson girl," born in the old *Life* in the nineties, had none of the then popular *fin de siècle* decadence—nor much real resemblance either to the spoiled and pudgy nymphs of upper-class America in that era. But life struggled manfully to imitate art. He did indeed reshape many an American girl and defoliate many a masculine lip and chin. The ideal Gibson images, displayed like pinups almost everywhere, have not yet been forgotten.

In this librarylike setting the photo department of the New York *World* carried on in 1909, as recorded by George Grantham Bain, himself a news photographer. Another photographer is coming down the stairs. The shelves on the back wall are stacked with rows and rows of glass plates. Joseph Pulitzer, the champion of "yellow journalism," had scarcely acquired the ailing *World* from Jay Gould in 1883 when he inaugurated the use of pictures with a diagram to illustrate a murder. Though he was not, strictly speaking, the very first to illustrate a daily newspaper, he was the first to make it pay. But his pictures were wood or zinc blocks made from sketches, not photographs at all. Although it had become possible to reproduce photographs in print by slow intaglio or lithographic methods, newspapers had a long wait for a method of printing photographs on a raised surface—the so-called "halftone" with its screen of fine dots—so that pictures could be included with type. In 1880 Stephen H. Horgan, a photographer whose work for the New York *Graphic* heretofore had been reproduced in their woodcuts, published the first dim newspaper halftone. But nothing much came of it for years. Pressmen scoffed, and publishers left halftones to art printers until 1897, when Horgan, now working for the *Tribune*, first printed photographs on high-speed presses. Then the rush was on, and photojournalism was born.

Under the ornate stairs of a New York El station in 1903 a Detroit Photographic Company man found this "characteristic" newsstand, which had many vanished magazines for sale— like *Collier's, Harper's Weekly, Leslie's, Vanity Fair*. Only two survivors, *Billboard* and *Scientific American*, are visible, and the general taste level seems about the same as in 1978, except that there are no girly magazines. Newspapers—and there were many more of them seventy years ago—were hawked on the streets by "self-employed" (so the newspapers stated) entrepreneurs like the one above, taken by Lewis Hine in the course of his crusade against child labor. The children bought their papers at wholesale, struggled for "territories," and were protected by the kindly New York State Newsboy Law from working longer than from 6 A.M. to 10 P.M. Men like Edison had begun as newsboys, asserted the newspapers. But for every success perhaps a dozen streetwise "little merchants" wound up in some kind of life of crime.

Literary Friends

Literary eminence at the close of the nineteenth century was shared, at least in the top drawer, by Mark Twain, Henry James, and William Dean Howells. Of these, Howells was for twenty-five years, from the mid-nineties to his death in 1920, the leading figure, the calm and beloved paterfamilias of American letters. From humble beginnings in Ohio he had shot forward to become, at thirty-four, the editor of the youthful *Atlantic Monthly*, the standard-bearer of realism in

the novels that poured from a prolific pen, a poet, a critic, and the first president of the American Academy of Arts and Letters—the last a position he held for the rest of a long, happy life. For his seventy-fifth birthday party at Sherry's in New York, President Taft came up from Washington. The most delightful of Howells's many friendships was that with Twain, recorded in a long series of letters. "You are really my only author," wrote Twain to Howells with typically boyish

exaggeration, "I am restricted to you. I wouldn't give a damn for the rest." Years later Howells paid back the tribute: "Emerson, Longfellow, Lowell, Holmes, I knew them all, and all the rest of the sages, poets, seers, critics, humorists. They were like one another and like other literary men. But Mark Twain was sole, incomparable, the Lincoln of our literature." Both men were sons of the Middle West, both started out as printer's devils—apparently as fine a highroad to knowledge and style as the high schools and colleges they never attended. Both also shared a delight in humor, to the point of farce. In these two uncaptioned photographs of Howells at work in his summer study at Kittery Point, Maine, one can almost imagine Mark Twain in the background, genially urging his highly respectable crony to pause for the strong waters that alone nourish genius—and Howells, of course, readily complying with the sober expression of a deacon.

While his reputation as Mark Twain grew apace, Samuel Clemens and his family spent their summers in Elmira, New York, the home of his wife Livy's family, the Langdons. They stayed at Quarry Farm, where his sister-in-law Susan Langdon Crane built him a little octagonal study, a fine place to work in peace compared with the busy life he led at home in Hartford. This undated, uncaptioned photograph from the Curtis Collection was taken at Quarry Farm; it seems to show nothing but a moment of relaxation for Twain and old John Lewis, the Cranes' tenant farmer. But there is more here than meets the eye. Years before, when Twain's hair was still flaming red and Lewis was a strapping man of forty-five, there had been a horrifying moment on these steps. Three of the family womenfolk were starting down the hill in a carriage, when suddenly the skittish horse ran away. The onlookers saw the carriage bouncing wildly in the air with each stone it hit; it was clear the rig would never make it around the sharp turn at the foot of the hill. The family stared in terror while Mark and his brother-in-law took off on foot in hopeless pursuit. But then at the bottom of the hill, driving a manure wagon, Lewis miraculously appeared. He saw what was happening. In seconds he maneuvered his wagon to make a narrow passage through which the galloping horse and its frightened passengers would have to pass. Then he jumped from his seat, made a flying leap, and with unerring aim seized the bit as the runaway raced by. And he brought the horse up standing. Twain was soon writing his friend Howells all about it—especially the aftermath: "When Lewis arrived the other evening, after saving those lives by a feat which I think is the most marvellous of any I can call to mind—when he arrived, hunched up on his manure wagon and as grotesquely picturesque as usual, everybody wanted to go and see how he looked.—They came back and said he was beautiful. It was *so*, too—and yet he would have *photographed* exactly as he would have done any day these past 7 years. . . ."

283

XIII. *On Stage*

The American professional theater is today at once the richest theater in the world, and the poorest. Financially, it reaches to the stars; culturally, with exceptions so small as to be negligible, it reaches to the drains.
— George Jean Nathan, 1922

The heart of show business, of course, was Broadway. In 1900 New York had upward of forty legitimate theaters—more than any other city in the world. But these were only the brightest of thousands of theaters scattered all across the Republic. In an age when the motion picture was nothing more than a jittering novelty, every tank town had its own opera house where, once in a while, a troupe would blow through and treat the residents to a little of the dazzle and pace of the big city. In the years following the Civil War, local stock companies began to dwindle as producers found it a surer draw to cultivate one famous actor and surround him with inexpensive nonentities. Men like John Drew, women like Lillian Russell, and the others on the following pages were the principals in the new star system. At the same time, as the era's delight with mechanism began to make itself shown on the stage, productions grew more complex and swollen: ships ran aground, men narrowly escaped being fed through buzz saws, locomotives raced through flames to pull scores of extras from blazing prairie villages. It was this love of spectacle that caused a Boston theatrical manager to despair of the meager look of his Last Supper scene. When his stage manager reminded him that there were, after all, only twelve Apostles, he snapped, "I know what I want! Gimme twenty-four!" As the productions grew more costly and difficult to manage, they fell prey to another of the era's specialties: combination in restraint of trade. In the late nineties a group of producers pooled their resources to form what came to be called the Syndicate, and thereby exercised enormous control over the profession. Some of the more powerful independent producers and performers—among them the actress Minnie Maddern Fiske—fought the Syndicate; many of the rest had to obey its dictates or go under. One contemporary observer wrote, "The theater has fallen into the clutches of sordid money-grubbing tradesmen, who have degraded it into a bazaar." But they couldn't have done it if the audiences hadn't loved the bazaar, and many who got their first view of the stage in those years echoed the view of the critic Walter Prichard Eaton. "It was a superb theater to be young in," he said, "[and] a great world to be alive in."

"Where the boys spend their money" is the sparse but eloquent explanation that accompanies the 1910 view of a St. Louis theater. When the boy springs his dime for a gallery seat, he will very likely see a vexed heroine in the same classic pose as that struck by the tragedian Mary Anderson at left. Her portrait was taken in 1883 by the New York photographer Napoleon Sarony, who was quite a showman in his own right. A flamboyant figure in his astrakhan cap and fur waistcoat, Sarony gradually abandoned the set-piece drama of posed pictures and brought a new ease and naturalness to portrait photography, which became evident in his later studies of theater folk.

The hugely successful *Becky Sharp*, an adaptation of Thackeray's *Vanity Fair*, opened in New York's Fifth Avenue Theater in 1899. Starring Tyrone Power senior (who stands, holding his hat, on the stairs) and Minnie Maddern Fiske (seated) in the title role, the play ran for two years before taking to the road. The fine view of the cast comes from the Byron studio, a unique family operation that recorded New York scenes from the 1880's to the 1930's. Joseph Byron was the best stage photographer of his day; his wife Florence printed his negatives, and his son Percy eventually joined him behind the camera. Minnie Fiske was the main draw for audiences who flocked to *Becky Sharp*. A lifelong performer—her stage career began at age three—she was, according to no less an authority than David Belasco, "one of the great artists, not only of this country, but of the world." She was instrumental in bringing Ibsen to startled American audiences. When she played Nora in *A Doll's House*, the spectators remained seated after the final curtain, until it dawned on them that the play had actually ended with a woman leaving her husband. Napoleon Sarony took this portrait of Minnie.

By all rights, the woman at left should never have stepped in front of Sarony's camera at all. She was a leader of English society in a time when such people simply did not go on the stage. But Lily Langtry—native of the island of Jersey, wife of a wealthy merchant, and a close friend of Edward VII— always did pretty much as she pleased. She first appeared on the London stage in 1882. The critics did not take her seriously, but the audiences did, and in the six years following her debut she amassed a fortune of half a million dollars. She was particularly well received in the United States, and returned the compliment by becoming an American citizen. Her most ardent admirer on this side of the Atlantic was probably Judge Roy Bean, the "law west of the Pecos," who claimed to have named his town of Langtry, Texas, after her. Although an unsentimental spokesman for the Southern Pacific insisted that Langtry had in fact been named for one of the line's construction managers, there is no doubt that Bean dispensed his capricious brand of justice from a saloon that he affectionately named the Jersey Lily.

Every actor wanted an "annuity part," a popular role the public identified with him and which he could brush off and run out during lean times. Joseph Jefferson had one of the most durable of them: for fifty years he was Rip Van Winkle. Jefferson, the scion of three generations of actors—his great-grandfather played alongside Garrick—first acted the part of Rip in 1859, when he was thirty. He was still going strong in 1896, when a New York photographer named B. J. Falk took this picture of him dressed as his narcoleptic hero.

Ample Charmers

Dressed in her costume for an 1894 opus called *The Grand Duchess*, Lillian Russell stares imperiously out at Sarony's camera. The daughter of a Clinton, Iowa, newspaper editor, she was born plain Helen Leonard but dropped that pallid name when, a long way out of Clinton, she started singing ballads in Tony Pastor's Bowery variety theater in 1880. Lusty, vivacious—and energetic—she delighted audiences, although critics tended to agree with a sour New York *Times* comment: "Singers, as a rule, are incompetent to act. Miss Russell furnishes no exception to the rule." She got married and divorced several times, and struck up a close friendship with Diamond Jim Brady, which seems to have been founded largely on their shared interest in gluttony. Together they stowed away immense meals; Brady generally kept ahead of her, but, he said, "for a woman, Nell done damn well." Thus she maintained the triumphant proportions of breast and hip that all the actresses of her era cultivated. Lillian Russell's last role was a very odd one indeed; Warren G. Harding, that astute judge of political ability, appointed her Assistant Commissioner of Immigration. She went to Europe, had a look around, and reported that we were letting too many foreigners into the country.

Although she did not enjoy the advantage of regular feasting with Diamond Jim, Bianca Lyons, the pensive woman at right—photographed by Chickering of Boston—managed to maintain the same daunting figure as Lillian Russell. Apparently, however, she had little else, for she never became famous.

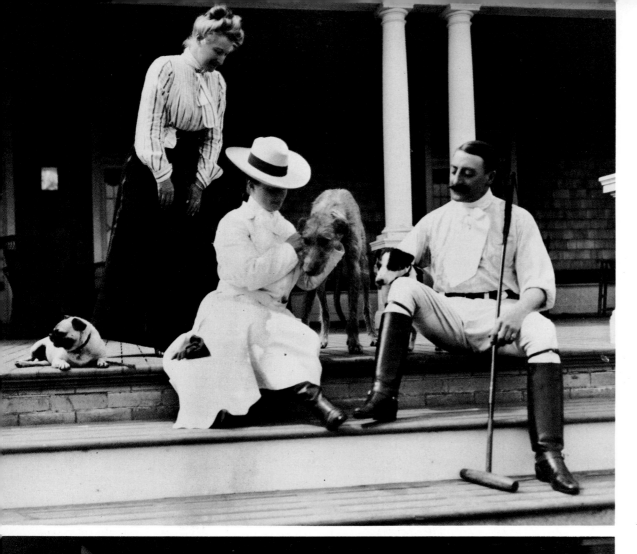

The Perfect Gentleman

"John Drew," said Booth Tarkington, "would play Simon Legree into a misunderstood gentleman, I believe." Clyde Fitch, who wrote many of the plays Drew appeared in, said that he was the only American actor who could be trusted to handle a silver dining service properly. Drew was known as the First Gentleman of the Stage. That title did not mean "foremost"; it meant, quite literally, the first. Before Drew, no actor—not even the great Edwin Booth—had been totally accepted in the upper reaches of American society. The son of a Philadelphia actor and theater manager, Drew was graduated from the Episcopal Academy and did not set foot on the stage until he was twenty. When he did, he quickly established himself as a player of exceptional grace and ease. He became a transitional figure in the theater, his relaxed style serving as a bridge between the melodramatic posturings of the 1870's and the naturalism of the modern theater. On the stage, said the New York *Herald* in 1904, "Mr. Drew is one person . . . blithe, debonair, talkative and enthusiastic. . . . As plain Mr. John Drew . . . he is quite another . . . serious, sedate and almost sad. More than that, if left to his own devices . . . he is as quiet as South Brooklyn at midnight . . . and he is as serious as a new policeman . . . self-contained, polished and silent." He had, however, a nice, dry sense of humor. When asked about reports that his nephew, John Barrymore, was helping out during the San Francisco earthquake, he said every word was true, but "it took an act of God to get him out of bed and the United States Army to put him to work." These pictures, taken by one of the tireless Byrons in 1902, show Drew—a tailor's dream—in his dressing room and, at left, in the library of Kyalami, his elegant Easthampton home. Above left, he chats with his wife Josephine and his daughter Louisa.

This limber quartet is a tiny fragment of the cast of *The Black Crook*, which was in its eighth New York revival when Sarony took the picture in 1893. The show had been put together in 1866 when a New York impresario suggested putting a European ballet troupe into a melodrama he had booked. The resulting amalgam of songs, dances, and an inane story loosely adapted from *Faust* was America's first successful revue. "The scenery is magnificent," said the New York *Tribune*, "the ballet is beautiful; the drama is—rubbish." But what the show lacked in drama it made up for in sheer spectacle and energy. It ran for a stupefying five and a half hours, and during that time the audi-

ence got to see a crystal grotto, "a hurricane of gauze," a villain carried off to hell, a dove transformed into Stalacta, the fairy queen, an "original and wonderful mechanical donkey," and—most important—the cancan. That scandalous dance made *The Black Crook* a memorable success. The show ran for seventeen months and made a profit of two hundred thousand dollars. Thousands of revues followed, and the winsome costuming at right was almost certainly created for two of them. All we know about them for sure is that the young woman—or possibly women—was photographed in the quaintly named Ye Rose Studio of Providence, Rhode Island, in 1904.

In the late 1840's New York theaters started featuring young women imitating famous statuary or portraying classical subjects—Venus rising from the waves, Psyche going to her bath. The New York *Herald* scolded: "The majority go because of depraved taste rather than pure love of art." Nevertheless, this uplifting device for getting undressed women on a stage was popular for years, and such tableaux vivants could be seen in any American city during the mid-

1880's, when a New York photographer named Naegli recorded these two classical scenes: Ganymede offering a cup to Venus and something entitled "Reconciliation." Vignettes like these represented the first regular exploitation of female sexuality on the legitimate American stage. The women, of course, were not naked—real skin was an extreme rarity in even the gamiest theater before the 1920's—but tights were quite sufficient to titillate and outrage the nineteenth century.

Prodigies

Among the youngest of the celebrities who posed for Sarony was the piano prodigy Josef Casimir Hofmann. Sarony photographed him standing by his piano—which bears a subtle reminder of the name of its New York manufacturer—during his first American tour in 1887. Hofmann was born near Cracow in 1876 and started playing a little over three years later. His career ran counter to those limned in the usual child-prodigy horror stories. After his first enthusiastically received American concerts the Society for the Prevention of Cruelty to Children kicked up a fuss, and an anonymous patron offered to take care of Hofmann's family until the boy was eighteen. Very much against his own wishes, young Josef was forced to abandon the concert stage for the intervening years.

Here is Enrico Caruso looking just like what he was—the foremost operatic tenor of his time at the height of his powers. Chickering took the picture in 1907, four years after the singer had made his American debut in *Rigoletto* at the Metropolitan Opera House in New York City. For nearly two decades Caruso remained the Met's reigning attraction. High-strung, flamboyant, and vigorous, Caruso loved America, though he was thoroughly disgruntled when he got caught in the San Francisco earthquake. But even then he knew how to take care of himself. It is said that, as he fled from his lurching hotel with the city shaking itself to pieces around him, he was followed by a servant clutching a warm towel for the great man's sensitive throat.

Temptresses

These women lived on the barren fringes of the theater—if, indeed, they could be said to be part of it at all—and yet the Library of Congress has more pictures of anonymous women like them than it does of the Lily Langtrys and the Lillian Russells. There are boxes and boxes of photographs, all innocently labeled "studies"; but a good number of them are large prints, doubtless intended for saloons and bachelor flats. The vintner's dream below was photographed in St. Louis in 1902 by the "studies" specialist F. W. Guerin. The solemn double-image figure toasting herself at right (despite a good deal of skillful retouching, she is remarkably racy for her day) is one of his many earnest tributes to Venus.

Mighty Men

The man straining at the pillar deserves a niche in show-business history not only for his vaudeville strong-man feats but also as Flo Ziegfeld's first great promotional success. Strapped for an act to rival the pull of Little Egypt's cooch dance at the 1893 Chicago world's fair, Ziegfeld hired a German named Eugene Sandow, who had been lifting weights for listless audiences in New York. Ziegfeld brought him to Chicago amid clouds of ballyhoo. Announcing that women who contributed three hundred dollars to charity could squeeze Sandow's muscles, Ziegfeld opened a totally revamped show. Sandow lifted pianos, let horses walk on him, wrestled drowsy lions—and by 1894, when B. J. Falk took this picture, he was one of the best-known men in America.

Unlike Sandow, Charles Murphy came to the vaudeville stage from the sporting arena. A crack bicycle racer, he had made himself famous and gained his nickname "Mile a Minute" in 1889 when, churning along behind a modified railroad coach, he did the distance in 57⅘ seconds. Carl J. Horner, a Boston photographer, took this picture of him vying with Tom Butler, another ace wheelman, on an ingenious machine designed to simulate race track conditions.

Anna's Girls

While Sandow earned Ziegfeld his first real money, Anna Held, whose cameo portrait appears at right, made his career. It was Anna who influenced him to stage a revue featuring beautiful girls. He met the Polish actress while she was singing—with little real distinction—in England in 1896. He brought her to America and set about generating the same sort of publicity that had sold Sandow. She received reporters in what Ziegfeld insisted was a replica of Marie Antoinette's

boudoir and, reclining in a negligee, told them she bathed daily in milk. Well before she made her debut in a farce called *The Parlor Match* her success was assured. "She would not be a 'sensation' at all," the New York *Times* complained, "if the idea had not been ingeniously forced upon the public mind that she is . . . naughty." In 1907, surrounded by fifty Anna Held Girls, like the wasp-waisted but sturdy women below, she romped through the first edition of *The Follies*

(Ziegfeld did not add his name to the show until 1911) in the rooftop garden of the New York Theater. The lavish show had cost Ziegfeld thirteen thousand dollars to mount —in a decade, he would be paying ten times that—and it was a tremendous success. When a beautiful girl in a lavish seashore number lost her bathing suit, a critic reported, "The sight so affected one young man in the audience that he gave vent to war whoops until the police put him out."

XIV. Simple Pleasures

The forests of America, however slighted by man, must have been a great delight to God; for they were the best he ever planted.

—John Muir

Puritanism and hedonism, contending through the centuries for the American soul, seem to have reached, some time around the 1880's, a kind of accommodation. Leisure, indeed pleasure, was acceptable if it was improving or educational. The summer camp clustered around the Chautauqua tents; the jolly steamboat excursion headed for the revival meeting. Such at least is the testimony of the camera. Most of our pictures of vacationers and travelers are the work of professionals, sent in for copyright with an eye on the stereoscopic, postcard, and travel-literature trade, but technological advances in the 1880's had swollen the thin ranks of the amateurs. One was the gelatin dry plate, which could be bought ready-made and quickly displaced the old-fashioned wet collodion plate, which had to be prepared on the spot and used at once. Many makes of hand-held cameras appeared to replace the enormous old tripod-mounted models. Then, in 1888, George Eastman, a dry-plate manufacturer, patented his simple, revolutionary Kodak. The early ones cost twenty-five dollars, no modest sum in that era, and held one hundred exposures; you sent them and the camera and ten dollars to Rochester, got back your prints and your camera completely reloaded. In the 1890's Eastman introduced flexible film, sold in light, compact rolls; and in 1900 he unveiled the most popular of all United States camera models, the box Brownie. As Edward Steichen once said, "No one has ever exhausted the potentialities of a Brownie." The sleeping camper opposite and the pictures on the three pages following are examples of what a skilled amateur could accomplish, even in the days before Eastman and his slogan, "You press the button, and we do the rest." The man who made them was Joseph J. Kirkbride (1842-1899), a bachelor physician from Philadelphia, son of the noted Dr. Thomas Story Kirkbride, a famous pioneer in the treatment of mental illness. At his father's instance, Joseph had received help in his photography from the noted Langenheim brothers; the younger doctor, an avid photographer, traveled widely in the United States and abroad. In the Library of Congress are eight big albums of Joseph's photographs devoted to two of his regular vacation haunts, Moosehead Lake in Maine and St. James City on Pine Island, near Fort Myers on the west coast of Florida. They are so full of fun and activity by large groups of Kirkbride's stylish friends that one hopes the doctor's other travel albums will some day turn up. It is no small added virtue that, unlike so many amateurs, he carefully captioned and dated his pictures.

Manifold were the joys of camping, especially if one's couch for the night were as carefully contrived as this one, photographed in 1888 in Maine by Dr. Kirkbride. His friend's head is protected by a nightcap and his body warmed by a fur-lined sleeping bag once used on the famous, ill-fated Greely Arctic expedition of 1881.

Unbelievable as their clothes may be for an outing in the Maine woods, the ladies have joined the gentlemen for a picnic dinner in this picture by Dr. Kirkbride. It was September 7, 1885, at the First Falls of the Socatean Stream, near Moosehead Lake, one of his favorite vacation places. The logistics required to produce table, dinner, and chairs in the wilderness, even with eight guides, must have been impressive. But the gentlemen, with the exception of their sports hats, are gotten up almost as formally as their wives. No genteel member of either sex ever went outdoors uncovered, for which a large industry, now moribund, rejoiced.

Normally, fishing may have been a man's sport, but Dr. Kirkbride's camera found an impressive exception in one of his guests at his winter retreat in St. James City, Florida, sometime in the mid-1880's. This sturdy angler was Mrs. Charles E. Allan of Glasgow, Scotland, posing with her two big tarpon—and the inevitable hat. The veteran angler at the right, photographed at some popular but unstated spot in the Adirondacks by Seneca Ray Stoddard in 1890, apparently finds a swallow-tailed coat just the thing for fishing.

In a long, adventurous life John Charles Frémont explored so widely that he became known as the "pathfinder of the West," played a major role in seizing California in 1846, ran as the first presidential candidate of the new Republican Party in 1856, fought in the Civil War, and made and lost fortunes in gold and California land. Not the least of his conquests was the heart of Jessie, the strong-willed sixteen-year-old daughter of Senator Thomas Hart Benton of Missouri, whom he married against her father's wishes in 1841. In this photograph of 1888 by a man named Aydelotte for "Reese's Photographic

Views," General Frémont, old, broke, but still proud, stands in front of one huge tree in a California grove. Jessie is on his left, their daughter on his right. The party has joined hands to demonstrate the tree's circumference. Under a tree nearby, Frémont had made his headquarters forty-two years before.

OVERLEAF: Bigness back east was a feature of resort hotels, not of trees. This Seneca Stoddard picture shows a medium-size establishment, Blue Mountain Lake House in the Adirondacks, about 1889. The usual crowd has turned out for the serious business of watching other guests arrive and depart.

313

No Plexiglas, no vista dome protects the sightseers in these two photographs, both probably taken by William H. Jackson. The jolly motorized charabanc above was the way to crane up at Manhattan's new skyscrapers in 1904, while the somewhat unsettling scene of 1899 at the right (don't look down!) was the greatest tourist attraction in California. Disneyland is tame stuff beside the vanished thrills of the Alpine Division of the Pacific Electric Railway, once the world's largest trolley and interurban system. You left Los Angeles in the big red PE cars for Pasadena, continuing up Echo Canyon to Rubio; there you transferred to an incline that climbed 3,500 feet, with all southern California spread out below. At the summit was the narrow-gauge Alpine open trolley, which twisted over 18 high trestles and 127 curves to the Alpine Tavern just below Mount Lowe, named for Professor Thaddeus S. C. Lowe, the daring Civil War balloonist who constructed the line in 1893. The tavern burned down in 1936, and shortsighted Los Angeles abandoned the line in 1938.

OVERLEAF: The need for the superlative, to be the highest, longest, best, and at all events biggest, burns with a steady flame in the American breast. This picture, copyrighted in 1907 from a Waterbury, Connecticut, address, but otherwise unidentified, is one from a pile of large prints in a ragtag-and-bobtail section of the Library of Congress's catalogued holdings called the Single Picture File. No one can argue with its claim to show the World's Greatest Sleigh Party. But would it not have been more fun to go in just one sleigh?

317

Wonders of Space

Though most middle-class Americans lived quiet lives in the Coolidge prosperity of the mid-twenties, there were nevertheless many delectable excitements paraded before them by the press: it was a simple pleasure to be shocked, vicariously, whether by flappers or bootleggers or the tragic predicament of Floyd Collins, trapped in a Kentucky cave. In person one could do the new crossword puzzles, tinker with a crystal set, or watch the complete eclipse of the sun of January 24, 1925, shown in these two photographs by Herbert E. French's National Photographic Company. President Coolidge studies the phenomenon with his usual dutiful boredom, below; his wife seems more interested. The notable photograph opposite is of William Jennings Bryan, thrice-defeated Democratic candidate for the presidency, the "Great Commoner" and, in matters of science and religion, the great fundamentalist. He told the photographer that "the eclipse is very much like the defeat of the Democratic Party; it is only temporary and the sun will soon shine again." But one wonders what he really thought as he peered through some exposed film. Perhaps very little. Six months later he would take on Clarence Darrow in the famous Scopes, or "monkey," trial, defending a literal teaching of the Bible in the Tennessee schools against the assaults of Darwinism and modern science. He would affirm his belief that the world was created in 4004 B.C., precisely; that Eve was made out of Adam's rib; and that a "big fish" had swallowed Jonah. Pious or irreverent, everyone lapped up the spectacle, then felt sorry when the true believer, his reputation eclipsed, died a week after the trial.

The earliest settlers in America had seen enough salt water to last a lifetime in cockleshells like the *Mayflower*; most of them were at pains never to go near it again. But "bathing," as it was genteelly described, grew in popularity in the late nineteenth century, although it cannot be said to have shown off the prevailing human body to advantage. In this 1888 photograph we cannot identify the gentleman in what looks like (but surely cannot be) B.V.D.'s, or anyone else except young Frances Benjamin Johnston, who is sitting on the gunwales of the little catboat nearest the unknown photographer. She is getting tanned, which was frowned on for ladies in the Gilded Age and accounts for the umbrellas at right.

Very few subjects in the time between the Civil War and World War I received more attention from photographers than the predictable marvels of fairs and expositions, which came in growing numbers after the success of the Philadelphia centennial exposition of 1876 and Chicago's "White City" of 1893. It was at the latter that the huge passenger-carrying wheel at left first appeared. Designed by and named after George Washington Gale Ferris, it reappeared in 1904 at the Louisiana Purchase Exposition in St. Louis, Missouri, where these stereographs were taken. It had thirty-six cars

and a diameter of two hundred fifty feet. The charming scene above looks past three fair visitors across a lagoon to Festival Hall. To plain people from farms and small towns, these expositions were fairylands, magic doors to science and the wonders of foreign lands. If the midways with their wild dancers and tame Indians distressed some visitors, they also delighted others. Out of the St. Louis fair came two cowboy riders, Will Rogers and Tom Mix; a minstrel boy from the Irish Village named John McCormack; and the song that is whistled to this day: "Meet Me in St. Louis, Louis."

The roller coaster, monarch of all amusement park rides, had scarcely been invented before it began to undergo fearsome refinements. This scary machine, elegantly called the "centrifugal pleasure railway" by its inventor, opened at Coney Island in 1901. William H. Jackson of the Detroit Photographic Company took this picture of it two years later. Quickly nicknamed the Loop-the-Loop, it became known by that name. Others went up in Chicago and Boston, but none of them were great moneymakers. For one thing, people were frightened of it. However many times its promoters rode through the loop holding full glasses of water to show the timid that not a drop spilled, the public remained leery. The ride did gain a reputation gaudy enough for the owners to charge people just to watch it, but even when there were riders, only four could be handled every five minutes, and few Loop-the-Loops survived the decade.

327

In the narrative of his first voyage Columbus wrote that "a great many Indians came to the ship today for the purpose of bartering their cotton, and *hamacas*, or nets, in which they sleep." The hammock, thus attested to be one hundred per cent American—whatever naval historians of other nations may claim to the contrary—reached its full flowering on the front porches of the nation in the closing years of the last century. Like everything else in the 1880's and 90's, this one has fringes, but the device is tricky nonetheless. A false move, and the occupant is on the floor, or sprawled over the potted palms. Our unknown gentleman, taken by an unknown photographer, is cheating, because he is employing a steadying foot, but he reminds us of the simplest pleasure of them all, a quiet afternoon doing nothing. If life was earnest, and the world outside a drowsy verandah was full of tumult, this was happiness as we remember it or imagine it to have been. Presently the newspaper will fall from the gentleman's hand, and he will drop off to sleep in the peace of long ago.

XV. Epilogue: Glimpses of a New Era

The pace was faster, the shows were broader, the buildings were higher, the morals were looser, and the liquor was cheaper; but all these benefits did not really minister to much delight.
— F. Scott Fitzgerald, 1926

Great wars, man is told when they come on, are fought to save ways of life. But what they generally do is bring them to an end. The First World War, in fact, seems to have put a period to the era examined in this book, an impression only heightened by photographs of the postwar years, a few of which are sampled in this chapter. America had long remained an optimistic country, built around the homestead and the large farm family, reasonably certain as to its morals, its duties, and its faith. The war left a people disillusioned, cynical, and eager to live for the day. On the old society, materialism laid a harsh and cheapening hand. Not everyone, as movie flashbacks would have us believe, danced the Charleston, drank bootleg gin, and "petted" in rumble seats—but millions forsook the old home, sold the old iron beds, moved to a flat, and lost contact with older values. By the end of the 1920's the once-rural people were almost sixty percent urban or lived in metropolitan areas. Millions bought automobiles, millions speculated in the stock-market boom, millions lived on the installment plan. Women moved out of the kitchen and achieved an emancipation that often turned to ashes, if we look to the divorce rate and the literature of the age of cynicism. Nevertheless, the twenties laughed at the older generation and looked pityingly at its handful of childhood friends who never left the old home town. Standardization was a steamroller. People who once played their own games and made their own amusements sat glued to the radio, whose entertainments quickly sought for and found the lowest common denominator. More and more they watched professional athletes instead of swinging a bat themselves. The movies, despite their gaudiness and their unreality, gave several generations their picture of what life should be. And in the period leading into a depression and another world conflict, America suffered government on scarcely any better a level than it was vouchsafed in the decade after the Civil War. As for photography, which is after all the subject of this book, the art leaped forward in great technological strides. Cameras were cheaper and easier to operate, film was fast and usable anywhere. Yet the product, somehow, was less distinguished than when one had to take infinite pains—or, to give voice to fugitive prejudice, it may be that the scenes before the lens were somehow less inspiring.

The self-consciousness of modern times reaches what is oratorically known as The Vanishing American in this faintly ludicrous photograph of Indians examining their negatives. They had taken part in one of the movies of Indian life made during one of several ethnological expeditions in the West financed by Rodman Wanamaker and led by an enthusiast named Dr. Joseph Kossuth Dixon, who took this picture. Total extermination having failed, romanticization was now to be tried. It turned out to be box office.

Where Lincoln's Army Marched

This army of midday ghosts, frightening and ludicrous at the same time, and unimaginable today, is the vanguard of the resuscitated Ku Klux Klan, marching down Pennsylvania Avenue on a fine day in 1925. Behind is the Capitol, where America of the 1970's lectures South Africans, Rhodesians, and other nations on tolerance and brotherhood. Founded during the excesses of Reconstruction and carpetbagger power to frighten newly freed blacks, the night-riding Klan by the twentieth century had all but died of its own futility. But in the unsettled years after World War I it rose again—especially in the Middle West—in what its leader Hiram Evans, a sometime cut-rate dentist from Dallas, called "aggressive warfare against Romanism, alienism, Bolshevism, and anti-Americanism of all kinds." The forty thousand members of the Invisible Empire shown here strode cheerfully, like so many Elks, past three hundred thousand fascinated spectators to the Washington Monument, where they lay down on the grass under threatening skies awaiting an evening ceremony. "Don't leave," a Kleagle told them, "it will not rain! God won't let it." But God did, and the cross-burning had to be postponed until the next day. Throughout the remainder of the decade, rain kept falling on the Klan's fortunes; enlightened opposition, American common sense, and scandals within the Klan caused its membership to dwindle from three million to a few hundred thousand. Bed-sheet sales declined. The sociologist John Mecklin predicted this disintegration as early as 1924. It would be due, he added, "to the essential local nature of the Klan, its singular lack of able or statesmanlike leaders, its planless opportunism and, above all, its dearth of great unifying and constructive ideals."

OVERLEAF: Like other parts of the rural United States, the farm country of the segregated South—where the Klan drew its main strength—had begun to change, but only in a few ways. In 1939, when Dorothea Lange took this "Tobacco Road" scene in Gordonton, North Carolina, the country store had installed modern gas pumps, but the road was still unpaved, the building unpainted, and the black man drank his soda pop outside on the porch.

The new woman burst upon America after the Great War in many sizes and shapes. A great many of them—almost a catalogue—are included in this panorama, which enshrines in history the Annual Bathing Girl Parade of 1920 at Balboa Beach, California, as copyrighted by one M. F. Weaver. It is one of a huge boxful of similar scenes from a dusty corner of the Library of Congress. To re-create the line of Aphrodites, start at the left, then lift the two pages and read across; end on the flap at right. From the evidence of the picture, there is no apparent winner. Perhaps no judge, having

The job of regulating the beginnings of radio broadcasting fell on, of all people, Herbert Hoover, Coolidge's conscientious Secretary of Commerce; he appears here in 1925, trying out what the caption calls "an ordinary listener's set." Hoover supported free-enterprise broadcasting but was distressed that advertisers would not limit themselves to giving their names and saying, he suggested, something like, "We would be glad to have your custom." His task of keeping stations on their assigned wavelengths was hard, one of the worst offenders being the Angelus Temple of the flamboyant evangelist Aimee Semple McPherson, who wired him in a rage to "order your minions of Satan to leave my station alone. You cannot expect the Almighty to abide by your wavelength nonsense." Below: Thomas A. Edison might not have been happy with the eventual uses made of the motion picture machine that he developed. In 1908, when this crowd filed into the Litchfield, Minnesota, opera house to see an Edison one-reeler, it was enough to see a picture move—just as, on the radio, no one cared so much about what was being said as that he had heard it. Innocence, however, does not last very long.

surveyed this dazzling set of costumes, could have made a choice. Nor is there any information about the baby or the "Spalding Maid" banners. Bathing suits and female figures improved rather abruptly in the twenties after the first nightmare of revelation brought about by the kind of swimwear flaunted here. In fact, the beauty contest itself was a product of the twenties, quite unthinkable to most women a decade or two before. Atlantic City's "Miss America" contest was born in 1921, became an institution, and today continues manufacturing instant Cinderellas. Some of them can even swim.

Some light years away in outlook and attitude from the nymphs on the preceding pages, these two young campaigners for equal rights are tipping their hats to a gentleman acquaintance. He seems to be struggling to repress a smirk. Gesture to gesture, equal to equal, that is the idea of the crusading Alice Paul, head of the National Woman's Party, where these two young women work. Of course, it has all been arranged beforehand for publicity, and posed for the delighted photographer from Washington's National Photo Service; the Capitol is nicely placed in the background. If hat-tipping by women never really caught on (because, among other things, it might have required extensive repairs to hairdos each time), a great many other more substantial changes revolutionized the lives of American women in the 1920's. A whole generation was being reared in a world of new morals, new jobs, new physical freedoms and, above all, new ambitions. That such a gulf could yawn so widely between the lady of, say, 1914, and the flapper of 1924, is one of those overnight, only partly explicable events—like the sudden youth rebellion of the 1960's, for example—whose reality photography makes so palpable.

E. O. Goldbeck, a San Antonio photographer, was proud
enough of his town to take the astonishing panorama of it
being displayed here. Few views demonstrate the phenomenon
of panoramic photography so splendidly as this one; the only
picture in the book (outside the Introduction) that is not part
of the Library of Congress collections, it is included through

the courtesy of Mr. Goldbeck himself. Four feet high and all of forty-eight feet long, the panorama was then the largest picture ever taken, and Goldbeck sent it to Philadelphia for the Sesquicentennial Exhibition of 1926. Apart from showing the viewer all he could possibly care to know about the topography of San Antonio, this photograph also reflects the vigorous spirit of boosterism that permeated the decade. Bigger was still better, and the women unfurling the picture in the field of wildflowers are doubtless as mightily proud as Mr. Goldbeck of their burgeoning city. And they would have seen nothing wrong with their field being paved over—which most likely happened as San Antonio kept on growing.

The Future Is Here

Leaning pensively on the neck of his pony, a cowboy watches his herd grazing on a diminishing stretch of pasture in front of the Dallas skyline of 1945. The American landscape had changed almost beyond imagining in the few decades that separate the crowded urban backdrop in this picture from the nineteenth-century image of the lone cowhand on the prairie. And photographic styles have changed, too. William Langley, who took the picture, doubtless posed his subject quite carefully to make a journalistic point— something that would scarcely have occurred to his counterparts in the last century. But if the irony is intentional, it is none the less valid for that, and the point is still a true one: America continues to watch—and to wonder if it can ever control—the enormous, awkward machines bequeathed her so confidently by the nineteenth century.

348

Acknowledgments

Whatever merit this book possesses belongs in the first instance to the great departed company of photographers who took these pictures, and in the second to the Library of Congress, which has preserved them in spite of heroic difficulties. Because of their inherent complexity, photographs cannot be organized into handy master or union catalogues, let alone be computerized. Neither could any one person inspect and replace millions of photoprints and negatives. What one needs is a guide with taste and experience, and this I was fortunate to find in the person of Shirley L. Green of Washington. I am much indebted to her, as I also am to Nelson Gruppo of New York, my other principal collaborator, who designed and laid out the book.

As a public institution, the Library of Congress plays no favorites and places its resources at the disposal of anyone who comes to study them, but it takes a fatherly interest in any long project. For such good will I thank especially Dr. Daniel Boorstin, the Librarian of Congress.

Early in the 1950's Paul Vanderbilt, then head of the Prints and Photographs Division, first aroused my interest in the historical breadth of its collections, and a few years later his successor, the late Edgar Breitenbach, took me on an eye-opening tour. During his active retirement and until just before his tragic death within the year, Dr. Breitenbach gave me more valuable advice. Two other knowledgeable veterans, Milton Kaplan and Alan Fern, were also very helpful. Mr. Fern is now director of the Research Department.

The present staff of Prints and Photographs was most hospitable, and I want to thank the present chief, Dale Haworth; Jerald Curtis Maddox, Curator for Photography; Jerry Kearns, head of the Reference Section; as well as Leroy Bellamy, Samuel Daniel, George Hobart, Beverly Brannan, Ford Peatross, Tom Beecher, Lenore Gift, and Elaine Canlas. To Betsy Betz, Pictorial Cataloguing Specialist, I owe the opportunity to read in manuscript her proposed book on the organization and cataloguing of the division's holdings. In the careful business of making prints and copy negatives, my needs were ably met by Marita Stamey and William Younger of the library's Photoduplication Department.

For kind assistance of various kinds I should also like to thank Don H. Berkebile, Maitland C. DeSormo, Walter S. Dunn, Jr., Donald C. Freeman, Mrs. C. E. Helfter, Neville Kirk, Laura E. Ludwig, John Rohdehamel, B. R. Van Name, and John H. White.

This book is a kind of specialized successor to an earlier volume, *American Album*. That book, which drew on many sources rather than one great one, was published in 1968 by Joan Paterson Kerr, Murray Belsky, and myself when we were working together on *American Heritage* magazine. Both my former co-authors generously aided this new venture. I have received every kind of cooperation from the staff of the American Heritage Book Division, especially its Editor-in-chief, Ezra Bowen, its Text Editor, Richard Folger Snow, copy editor Beatrice Gottlieb, and researchers Jane Colihan and Myra Mangan.

Once again I have enjoyed the quiet encouragement and sensible advice of my good friend Joseph J. Thorndike, Jr., who has been my colleague in the business of pictures, magazines, and books for a steady forty years.

Library of Congress Cataloging in Publication Data

United States. Library of Congress. Prints and
Photographs Division.
America's yesterdays.

Includes index.
1. United States—History—Pictorial works.
2. United States—Social life and customs—Pictorial
works. I. Jensen, Oliver Ormerod, 1914-
II. Green, Shirley L. III. Title.
E178.5.U54 1978   973'.022'2   78-18426
ISBN 0-8281-3074-4
ISBN 0-8281-3073-6 deluxe

Library of Congress Negative Numbers

Negatives are listed left to right, then top to bottom, by pages or, when indicated, by spreads (*e.g.,* 20-21). For simplicity's sake, the prefix LC has been omitted from all numbers. The prefixes USZ6 and USZ62 indicate copy negatives; others mark original negatives. Missing numbers were unavailable at press time.

Cover G9-149066-A
Front Endpaper C8101-237
Back Endpaper USZ62-29390
Title Page J698-4923
Contents Page USZ62-63602
6 B2-3865
7 USZ62-1819; 17832; 431720
8 BH821-6619; B8151-10056; M.C.DeSormo*; Robert A. Weinstein*
9 J698-8751; USZ62-63530; USZ62-45769; USZ62-53123
10-11 B2-2083-11; USZ62-56733; missing; missing; USZ62-50647
12 USZ62-50647
14-15 D4-70366
16-17 USZ62-63423
18-19 USZ62-63424
20-21 USZ62-63446; USZ62-63445
22 USZ62-34842
23 USZ62-60818
26-27 USZ62-30126
28 USZ62-63419
29 USZ62-57838
30 USZ62-65209
31 USZ62-63425
32-33 USZ62-63421
34 USZ62-20358
36-37 V271-188; USZ6-16
38-39 V272-22; USZ62-50744
40-41 USZ62-63447
42-43 USZ62-29482
44 USZ62-33488
45 USZ62-45049
46-47 D4-70072
48 USZ62-63665
49 USZ62-63664
50-51 USZ62-63677
52 USZ62-28706
54 USZ62-46805
55 USZ62-27428
56-57 USZ62-63517; missing
58 USZ6-18
59 D4-70776
64 USZ62-16274; USZ62-23643; USZ62-5433; USZ62-16277
65 USZ62-57701
66-67 USZ62-63523; D4-14754
68 USZ62-63515
69 USZ62-63521
70-71 USZ62-63422; USZ62-28862
72-73 USZ62-63522; USZ62-63514
75 USZ62-63669
78-79 G9-151923-A; USZ62-56222
80 G9-137775-A
81 G9-153770-A

82-83 G9-118625-A
84 USZ62-56437
85 USZ62-63595
86 USZ62-63560
87 USZ62-63604
90-91 USZ62-63513
92 B2-2576-5
93 F8-19051
94 D4-17557; D4-17558
95 D4-17561
96-97 USZ62-13060
98 USZ62-63418
100-101 USZ62-63463
102 J698-100025
103 USZ62-63465
104-105 USZ62-1773; USZ62-63567
106 USZ62-63427; USZ62-63430
107 USZ62-63432; USZ62-63429; USZ62-63428; USZ62-63431; USZ62-63434; USZ62-63433
108-109 B2-2072-2; USZ62-63443
110-111 B2-603-7; USZ62-34094
112 USZ62-63458
113 USZ62-53047
114-115 USZ62-63450; USZ62-63452; USZ62-63451; USZ62-63453; USZ62-63454
118 USZ62-63543
119 USZ62-63542
120-121 USZ62-30353; USZ62-63670
122-123 USZ62-14544; missing
124 USZ62-63548
125 USZ62-63608
126 USZ62-63654
128-129 USZ62-63505; USZ62-63494
130-131 USZ62-63414; USZ62-63616
133 J694-359
134-135 USZ62-63629; USZ62-63415
136 USZ62-63495; USZ62-63493; USZ62-63496
137 USZ62-63501
138-139 USZ62-63416
140 USZ62-14282
141 USZ62-63652; USZ62-63653
142-143 B2-2779-4
144-145 USZ62-52381
146-147 USZ62-19579
148 USZ62-62749
150 USZ62-58914
151 USZ62-63596
152 USZ62-63598
153 USZ62-63536
154-155 USZ62-63603
156 USZ62-28023
157 USZ62-63534
158 USZ62-19557
159 USZ62-26270; USZ62-63572
160 USZ62-63533

161 USZ62-63532
162 USZ62-26261
163 W85-26
164 USZ62-63575
165 USZ62-63573
166 J694-289
167 J694-301
168 USF34-44765E
169 USF33-30577-M2; USF33-20861-M5
170 D6-87
171 B2-3922-5
172-173 USZ62-20622; USZ62-63509
174-175 USZ62-22484; USZ62-56638
176-177 USZ62-63413
178-179 B2-3894-6
180 F31-146
182 K2-37
184 D4-71124
186-187 USZ62-63647
188 USZ62-63558
189 USZ62-63466
191 USZ62-63576
192 USZ62-29478
193 USZ62-63621
194 USZ62-33686
195 USZ62-63645
196-197 USZ62-63678
198-199 USZ62-63681
201 USZ62-63557
205 USZ62-63562; USZ62-63554; USZ62-63552; USZ62-63553
209 USZ62-63555
210 USZ6-262
211 USZ62-63549
213 USZ62-41860; USZ62-41861; USZ62-26584; missing
214 USZ62-63502
216 USZ62-63651
217 USZ62-63492
220 USZ62-63607
221 USZ62-63561
222 USZ62-63716
223 USZ62-63674
225 F81-35427
226-227 C8-6
228 USZ62-63461
229 J698-1202
230-231 USZ62-50067; USZ62-45701
232 USZ62-63436; USZ62-63435; USZ62-63436; USZ62-63435
233 USZ62-63439; USZ62-63435; USZ62-63438; USZ62-63437; USZ62-63440; USZ62-63441
234-235 F81-36049
236 USZ62-19402
237 USZ62-41757
240-241 USZ62-63620
242-243 USZ62-63672
244-245 USZ62-63497; USZ62-63488
246 USZ62-63545; USZ62-63546
247 USZ62-63679
250 USZ62-63675
252 USZ62-4820
253 USZ62-29513
254 USZ62-46435
255 USZ62-63668

256-257 USZ62-8769; USZ62-52082
258-259 B2-2369-12; B2-2377-16; USZ62-22190
260-261 USZ62-63658; USZ62-53177
262 B2-4215-16
263 B2-3093-5
264-265 USZ62-63644; USZ62-63713
266-267 USZ62-63660
269 USZ62-63648
270-271 J698-81601
272 J698-90061
273 USZ62-4556
274 J698-6586
275 USZ62-40490; USZ62-63643
276-277 USZ62-55819
278-279 USZ62-45842; D401-16161
280-281 USZ62-12932; USZ62-61300
282-283 USZ62-60538
284 USZ62-29157
285 USZ62-63582
286-287 USZ62-63624; USZ62-63617
288 USZ62-63623
289 USZ62-63622
290 USZ62-63581
291 USZ62-63626
292 USZ62-63580; USZ62-63579
293 USZ62-62700
294-295 USZ62-55573; USZ62-55590; USZ62-55589
296-297 USZ62-63632; USZ62-63676
298 USZ62-63610
299 USZ62-63625
300 USZ62-63618
301 USZ62-25086
302 USZ62-63600
303 USZ62-55161
304-305 both USZ62-5465
306 USZ62-25362
308-309 USZ62-63613
310 USZ62-25359
311 USZ62-63592
312-313 USZ62-63586
314-315 USZ62-34578
316 D4-17555
317 USZ62-63578
318-319 USZ62-63588
320 F8-34016
321 F8-34014
322-323 USZ62-63635
324 USZ62-63547
325 USZ62-63544
326-327 D4-9181
330 D6-48
332-333 F81-36635
334-335 USF34-19911E
336 F81-34855
337 USZ62-63666
344-345 F81-36303
346-347 Goldbeck Collection,*
348-349 USZ62-63657

*not Library of Congress

Index

Numbers in italic type refer to pictures

A

Adams, Henry, 53
Adams, John Quincy, 187
Adirondack Mountains, 13, 28
  resort hotel in, *314-315*
Aerial Experiment Association, 81
airplanes, *78-79*
  Curtiss-Wright engine, *79*
Alcott, Louisa May, 269
American Academy of Arts and Letters, 280
American Stereoscopic Company, *209*
Anderson, Marian, 196
Anderson, Mary, *285*
Annapolis, *244-245*
Atlantic Monthly, 280
Ausable Chasm, *12*, 13
  boat ride to foot of the rapids, *12*
Austen, Ramie, *4*
Aydelotte, *312-313*

B

Bailey, Dix & Mead, *148*
Bain, George Grantham, 7, 10, *10*, *44-45*, *92*, *108-109*, 129, *142-143*, 171, *260-261*, *263*, *266-267*, *276-277*
Bain News Service, 7, 9, *10*, 171
Baldwin, F. W. ("Casey"), 82
Barrymore, John, *292*
Barton, Clara, 7, 85
baseball, in schools, *224-225*
Bean, Judge Roy, 288
Becky Sharp, *286-287*
Beecher, Catharine, 181
Beecher, Henry Ward, 181
Beecher, Isabel, 181
Belasco, David, 286
Bell, Dr. Alexander Graham, 7, 11, 78, *80*, 81, *82-83*
  hydrofoil designed by, *82-83*
  tetrahedral cells of, 81
Bell, C. M., *105*
Benét, Stephen Vincent, 149
Benton, Thomas Hart, 312
Berkman, Alexander, *260-261*, *262-263*
Bide-a-Wee home for animals, 265
Bird, Emma Marie and Grace, *182*
Black Crook, The, *294-295*
Black Hills, the
  Spearfish Falls, *29*
Blackfoot chiefs, *154-155*
Booth, Edwin, *292*
Booth, Evangeline, *265*
Booth, William, 265
Borglum, Gutzon, 269
Boston, Mass., *90-91*
Boston Public Library, Board of Trustees of, *226-227*
Botts, Benjamin, 187
Botts, John Minor, and family, *186-187*
Brady, Diamond Jim, *291*
Brady, Mathew, 7, 10, 8, *186-187*
Brandeis, Louis, 229
Breitenbach, Dr. Edgar, 7-8
Browne, Carl, *256-257*
Bryan, William Jennings, 51, 114, 120, *321*
Bryce, James, 13, 215
  American Commonwealth, The, 13, 99
Bryn Mawr College, 221
Buffalo, N. Y., *20-21*
Burr, Aaron, 187
Burrough, John, 76
Butler, Tom, *303*

Butler, William Allen
  "Nothing to Wear," 104
Butterfield, D. W., *16-17*
Byron, Joseph, and family, *286-287*, *292-293*

C

Calamity Jane, 36
California
  Alpine trolley of the Pacific Electric Railway, *317*
Cape Horn, 49
Carlisle Indian Industrial School (Pennsylvania), *154-155*
Carlyle, Thomas, 35
Carnegie, Andrew, 22, *133*, 215, 226
Caruso, Enrico, *299*
Carver, George Washington, 167
Cascade Mountains, 31
Catton, Bruce, 42
Central Park (N.Y.C.), *26-27*
Charter Oak, the (Hartford, Conn.), 16
Chicago
  World's Columbian Exposition, 68, 273, 302
Chickering, Elmer, *90-91*, *291*, *299*
child labor, 131, 144
  New York State Newsboy Law, *278*
Chinese settlers, *174*, *175*
Choate, J. N., *154-155*
Choate, Joseph, 229
Cincinnati *Enquirer*, 141
Cincinnati levee, *46-47*
Civil War, 7, 18, 39, 53, 187, *242-243*, 253
Clay, Henry, 106
Clemens, Samuel. *See* Twain, Mark
Cleveland, Frances Folsom, *103*, 105
Cleveland, Grover, 99, 103, 104, 106, 229
Clinedinst, B. M., *114-115*
cog railways, 11, 15
Comstock, Anthony
  Morals Versus Art, 272
Coney Island, *94-95*, *326-327*
Connecticut River, *14-15*
Coolidge, Calvin, 108, 269, *320*, 337
Corcoran School of Art, 271
Coxey, Jacob Sechler, *257*
Coxey's army, 256
Curtiss, Glenn, 78, *79*, 81
Custer, Gen. George A., 28, 123
Czolgosz, Leon, 101

D

Daniel, Josephus, 7
Darrow, Clarence, 320
Daughters of the American Revolution, *196-197*
Davis, Jefferson, 187
Day, F. Holland, 9
Deadwood, Dakota Territory, 36
Delano, Jack, *168*, 169
Depew, Chauncey, *108*
Detroit Photographic Company, 8, 10, *14-15*, *23*, *66-67*, *94-95*, *184*, *278-279*, *326-327*
Dewey, Adm. George, 9, 123
Dewey, John, 215
Dickens, Charles, 127
Dixon, Dr. Joseph Kossuth, *330*
Doll's House, A, 286
Doubleday, Maj. Gen. Abner, 243
Drew, Daniel, 20
Drew, John, *285*, *292-293*
Du Bois, W. E. B., *164-165*
Duffy, Rev. Francis P., *178-179*
Dunne, Finley Peter, 215
Dwight, Timothy, 215

E

Eaton, Walter Prichard, 285
Eddy, Peter, *10-11*
Edison, Thomas A., *76-77*, 337

Edison electric car, *76-77*
Edison Laboratories, 232
Edward VII, 288
Elder, Samuel J., *132*
Eliot, Charles William, 216, 225
Ellis Island, immigrants at, *170*
Erie Canal, 20
Ettor, Joseph J., *259*
Evans, Hiram, 332

F

Fabyan's, *10-11*
Fairbanks, Charles Warren, 197
Fairbanks, Mrs. Charles Warren, *196-197*
Falk, B. J., *4*, *70-71*, 289, *302*
Fall, Albert, 141
Farm Security Administration, *168-169*
Farnsworth, Emma Justine, *180*
Fellows Company, *213*
Fenton, Roger, 7, 10
Fern, Alan
  Viewpoints, 8
financial center, New York City, *70-71*
  American Stock Exchange, *71*
  old Curb Exchange, *70-71*
Fisk, Jim, 20
Fiske, Minnie Maddern, 285, *286-287*
Fitch, Clyde, 292
Fitzgerald, F. Scott, 331
Ford, Henry, 76
Frémont, Jessie Benton, *312-313*
Frémont, Gen. John Charles, 108, *312-313*
French, Herbert E., *11*, *234-235*, *320*, *321*
French and Indian Wars, 28
Frick, Henry Clay, 23, *260-261*
Fuller, Melville Weston, *228*

G

Galveston hurricane
  aftermath of, *84*, 85, *86*, *88*
  re-creation of, in Coney Island theater, *94*
Garfield, James A., 99
Geer & Bricker, *107*
Genthe, Arnold, 10
  portrait of John D. Rockefeller by, *58*
Gerry Society, 129
Gerson sisters, *183*
Gibbs, George, *270-271*
Gibbs, Josiah Willard, 36
Gibson, Charles Dana, *275*
Gibson girl, *275*
Gilman, Daniel Coit, 214, 215
Goering, Hermann, 7
Goethals, Col. G. W., 75
Goldbeck, E. O., *346-347*
Goldman, Emma, 260, *262*
Gompers, Samuel, 258
Grabill, J. C. H., *29*, 36, *52*, *174*
Green, Shirley L., 8
Gould, Jay, 277
Grant, Ulysses S., 99, 112, 251
Graves, C. H., *175*, *221*
Greeley, Horace, 250, 251
Green, W. A., *88*
Griffith & Griffith, 85
Grosvenor, Gilbert H., 81
Guerin, Fritz W., *247*, *300-301*

H

Hamilton, Alexander, 244
Hancock, John, 127
Hand, Learned, 229
Harding, Warren G., 226, 291
Harrison, Benjamin, 99, 104, 106
Harrison, Benjamin
  children named for, *106-107*
  inauguration of, *98*
Harrison, Caroline Scott, *104*
Harrison, William Henry, 99

Hart, Alfred A., 35, 39
Hart, William S., 232
Harvard University, 216, 225
Havens, O. Pierre, 156, *159*
Hawthorne, Nathaniel, 23
Hayes, Lucy, 99
Hayes, Rutherford B., 99
Haynes, F. Jay, 35
Hearst, Sen. George, 129
Hearst, Mrs. Phoebe Apperson
  library in home of, *128-129*
Hearst, William Randolph, 129
Held, Anna, *304*, *305*
Hemingway, Ernest, 42, 269
Heyn and Heyn & Matzen, 153
Hickok, James Butler ("Wild Bill"), 36
Hicks, Edward, 13
Higginson, Thomas Wentworth, 253
Hine, Lewis Wickes, 9, *130-131*, 135, *138-139*, *144-145*, *146-147*, *176-177*, 278
Hobart, Garret Augustus, *100-101*
Hofmann, Josef Casimir, *298*
Holmes, Oliver Wendell, 201, 229, 252
Holyoke, Mass., *14-15*
Homestead (Pa.) steel plant, *22*
  strike at, *22-23*, 260
Hoover, Herbert, 66
Hoover, J. Edgar, 262
Hope Diamond, *175*
Horgan, Stephen H., 277
Horner, Carl J., *303*
Houseworth, Thomas. *See* Lawrence, George
Howe, Julia Ward, 252
Howe, Samuel Gridley, 252
Howells, William Dean, *280-281*
Hunnewell Arboretum, *221*
Huxley, Thomas, 215

I

immigrants at Ellis Island, *170*
Indians, 148, *150-155*, *330*
Industrial Workers of the World, *176-179*, *258-259*, 258-259, *260-261*, 262

J

Jackson, William H., 8, 10, 35, *94-95*, 316, *317*, *326-327*
James, Henry, 53, 269, 280
Jarvis, J. F., *256-257*
Jefferson, Joseph, 127, 289
Johns Hopkins University, 215
Johnson, Andrew, 99
Johnson, Samuel, 181
Johnston, Frances Benjamin, *2-3*, 9, *10*, *102*, 103, *128-129*, *133*, *136-137*, *166-167*, 214, *222-223*, *244-245*, *270-271*, *272*, 273, *274*, *322-323*
Johnston, J. S., *26-27*, 237

K

Käsebier, Gertrude Stanton, 9, *183*
Keller, Helen, 81
Keystone View Company, *124*
Kinsey, Darius, *31*, 68
Kirkbride, Dr. Joseph J., *306*, 307, *308-309*, 310
Kirkbride, Dr. Thomas Story, 307
Knox, Henry, 244
Ku Klux Klan, 157, *332-333*
Kurtz, William, *112-113*

L

Lake George, N. Y., French Point at, *28*
Lange, Dorothea, *334-335*
Langenheim brothers, 307
Langley, Samuel Pierpont, 78
Langley, William, *348-349*
Langtry, Lily, 288
Lavelle, Monsignor Michael Joseph, *178-179*

Lawrence, George, *192*
    and Thomas Houseworth, *34, 55*
Lewis, John, *282-283*
Library of Congress, *6-7, 9-11*
    Prints and Photographs Division, *7-11*
    copyright collection, *10*
    Guide to the Special Collections, *8*
Lincoln, Abraham, *106, 157, 251*
Littleton View Company, *205*
Long Beach, Cal., oil fields at, *60-63*
Longworth, Alice Roosevelt, *102*
Longworth, Nicholas, *103*
Look magazine, *10*
Louisiana Purchase Exposition (St. Louis), *324-325*
Lowe, Thaddeus S. C., *316*
Lyons, Bianca, *291*

M

McCormack, John, *325*
McCosh, James, *216, 217*
MacDonald, Pirie, *275*
McGrory and Company (Atlanta), *158*
McIntosh, Burr, *120*
McKim, Mead and White, *226*
McKinley, William, *2-3, 101, 103, 120*
McLean, Edward Beale ("Ned"), *141*
McLean, Evalyn Walsh, *140, 141*
McLean, Vinson Walsh, *140-141*
McPherson, Aimee Semple, *337*
Martha's Vineyard, paddle steamer at, *36-37*
Mecklin, John, *332*
Melander, *213*
military, the. *See also* wars
    Annapolis, *244-245*
    the cavalry between wars, *238-239, 240-241*
    Gettysburg memorial service, *242-243*
    West Point, *244-245*
mining, *66, 129*
    silver miners, *66*
Mix, Tom, *325*
Mole, Arthur S., *248-249*
Mont Pelée eruption, re-creation of, *95*
Moody, Dwight L., *255*
Morgan, J. Pierpont, *120, 132, 273*
Mormon survivors of trek across the plains and mountains, *50-51*
Morris, William, *275*
Morton, Levi P., *106*
Mount Holyoke College, *221*
Mount Rainier, *30*
Mount Rushmore, *269*
Mount Tom, *14-15*
Mount Vernon, Va., *18-19*
Mount Washington, *10-11*
mourning prints, *190-191*
Muir, John, *307*
Murphy, Charles, *303*

N

Nast, Thomas, *275*
Nathan, George Jean, *285*
National Geographic Society, *81*
National Photo Service, *93, 344-345*
National Photographic Company, *225, 320, 321*
National Woman's Party, *345*
Negroes, *156-169*
New York City
    Central Park, *26-27*
    elevated railroad, *72-73*
    financial center, *70-71*
    Lower East Side of, *171*
    police department, *230-231*
    post office building in, *237*
New York *Tribune*, *251*
New York *World*, photo department of, *276-277*
Newell, R., & Son, *134-135*

Niagara Falls, *13*
    honeymoon couples at, *184*
Norton, Charles Eliot, *216*
Notman, William, *218-219*

O

Ogden, Robert C., *133*
oil fields at Long Beach, Cal., *60-63*
Oklahoma District land rush, *74*
Osler, William, *215*
Otis Elevator Company, *20*

P

Page, Walter Hines, *215*
Paine, Albert Bigelow, *269*
Panama Canal, *48*
    construction of, *75, 120*
    opening of, *75*
parades and politics, *110-111*
Paradise Glacier of Mount Rainier, ice cave in, *30*
Parker, Alton B., *114-115*
Parker, G., *104*
Paul, Alice, *345*
Pearl Harbor, *244*
Photo-Secession group, *183*
Pickford, Mary, *232*
Pierson, H. F., *96-97*
Pittsburgh, Pa., *22*
Plumbe, John, Jr., *54*
Plymouth, N. H., *23*
police department
    excerpts from *The Life of an American Policeman*, *232-233*
    of New York City, *230-231*
Pollock, Charles, *72-73*
Pond, C. L., *20-21*
post office buildings, in Searsburg, Vt., and New York City, *236-237*
Power, Tyrone, Sr., *286-287*
Pratt, Richard Henry, *154*
Prince, George, *125*
Princeton University, *216, 224*
Pulitzer, Joseph, *277*
Purdy, J. E., *126, 216, 220*
Pure Food and Drug Law, first, *255*
Pyle, Howard, *274*

R

railroads
    along tracks of Chicago, Rock Island & Pacific, *32-33*
    construction of Central Pacific, *39*
    engineer corps of Deadwood Central Railroad, *52*
    four-wheel switching engine, *38-39*
    freight car, *56-57*
    Grand Rapids and Indiana, *42*
    Nashville & Northwestern, *39*
    New York Central, *108*
    station at Petoskey, Mich., *42-43*
Rau, William H., *88-89*
Red Cross, *10, 85*
Richardson, James O., *244-245*
Riis, Jacob, *130*
Rinehart, Frank, *150-151, 152-153*
Rockefeller, John D., *58-59, 133*
    Cleveland home of, *59*
    portrait of, by Arnold Genthe, *58*
Rockett, Perley Fremont, *123*
Roebling bridge (Cincinnati), *46-47*
Rogers, Will, *325*
roller coaster, *326-327*
Roosevelt, Theodore, *9, 27, 99, 101, 103, 114, 116-119, 120, 123, 225, 260*
Royce, Josiah, *215*
Russell, Andrew J., *35, 39*
Russell, Lillian, *285, 290*

S

St. Patrick's Cathedral (New York City), *178-179*
Salvation Army, *265*
San Antonio, Tex., *346-347*
Sandow, Eugene, *302*
San Francisco shipyard, launching at, *55*
Sarony, Napoleon, *8, 285, 286, 288, 290, 294-295, 298*
Savage, Charles R., *35*
Schiller, William, *87*
school
    company-owned, for employees' children, *223*
    public elementary, *222*
Scopes trial, *320*
Seymour, Horatio, *112-113*
sharecroppers, *160-161*
Sherman, Sen. John, *53*
Sherman, Gen. William Tecumseh, *53*
Shriners, *198-199*
Sierra Nevada, crossing the, *34*
Singley, B. L., *124, 162*
Sioux Indians, *148, 150-151, 152-153*
Sitting Bull, *148*
Smith, Joseph, *50-51*
Smith, Preacher, *36*
Smithsonian Institution, *78*
Society for the Prevention of Cruelty to Children, *129, 299*
Spanish-American War, *122-123, 162, 163, 246, 247*
Spearfish Falls, in Black Hills of South Dakota, *29*
Spencer, Herbert, *53*
Spofford, Ainsworth Rand, *9*
Steele, F. M., *32-33, 189*
Steichen, Edward, *183, 307*
stereographs, *10*
stereoscopic pictures, *200-213*
Stevens, John, *75*
Stieglitz, Alfred, *183*
Stoddard, Seneca Ray, *8, 13, 28, 193, 244-245, 311, 314-315*
Stowe, Harriet Beecher, *181*
Strohmeyer and Wyman, *194*
Stuart, Gen. J. E. B., *187*
Sullivan, Annie, *81*
Sullivan, "Big Tim," *108-109*
Supreme Court of the United States, Chief Justices of, *228-229*
symbolic photography, *124-125, 247, 248-249*

T

Taft, William Howard, *111, 120-121, 132, 229, 280*
Talbot, C. A. P., *126*
Tammany Hall, *275*
    ballot-box stuffers at, *108-109*
Tangen, Ed, *85*
Tarbell, J. H., *157, 160-161*
Teapot Dome scandal, *141*
tenement apartment, *130-131*
Thompson, Mills, *270-271*
Thorpe, Jim, *154*
Tingley, G. E., *24-25*
Toles, H. E., *30*
tornado aftermath, *87*
trolley cars, open, *45*
    learning to board, *44*
Troth, Henry, *9*
Turner, Frederick Jackson, *215*
Tuskegee Institute, *133, 166, 169*
Twain, Mark, *268, 269, 280, 282-283*
Tweed, Boss, *275*

U

Underwood & Underwood, *114-115, 173, 188*
United States Steel Corporation, *22, 223*

V

Vanderbilt, Cornelius, *20, 108*
Vanderbilt, Paul, *8*
    Guide to the Special Collections, *8*
Van Name, Dr. Willard Gibbs, *36-37*
Vidor, King, *85*

W

Walsh, Tom, *141*
Wanamaker, Rodman, *331*
wars
    Civil War, *7, 18, 39, 53, 187, 242-243, 253*
    Spanish-American War, *122-123, 162, 163, 246, 247*
    World War I, *75, 262, 331*
    World War II, *10*
Washington, Booker T., *133, 165, 166*
Washington, D. C.
    Patent Office, *54*
Washington, George, *18, 106, 244*
Washington, Col. John Augustine, *18*
Washington, John H., *166*
Washington Elm, the (Cambridge, Mass.), *16*
Washington *Post*, *141*
Webster, Daniel, *23, 229*
wedding picture, *185*
Weldon, Catherine, *148*
Wellesley College girls, *221*
Werner, G. A., *69*
West Point, *244-245*
White, Andrew D., *215*
White, Clarence, *9*
White, Edward Douglass, *229*
Whiting View Company, *205*
Whittier, John Greenleaf, *16*
    "Wood Giant, The," *16-17*
Whittier Pine, The (Squam Lake, N. H.), *16-17*
Wiley, Dr. Harvey, *254*
Wilman's Peak in the Cadet Mountains (Washington), *31*
Wilson, Woodrow, *120, 215, 216*
Wolcott, Marion Post, *169*
Women's Christian Temperance Union, *196*
Woolley, Mary Emma, *220*
World War I, *75, 262, 331*
World War II, *10*
World's Columbian Exposition, *68, 273, 302*
Wright Brothers, *7, 11, 79, 92*
    bicycle shop of, *163*
Wyeth, N. C., *275*

Y

Yale University, *132, 218-219*
Young, Brigham, *50*
Young, R. Y., *118-119*

Z

Zahner, M. H., *86*
Ziegfeld, Florenz, *302, 304-305*
Ziegfeld Follies, The, *305*